Changing How You Manage and Communicate Change

Focusing on the human side of change

Soft Skills for IT Professionals

Changing How You Manage and Communicate Change

Focusing on the human side of change

NAOMI KARTEN

Soft Skills for IT Professionals

IT Governance Publishing

IT Governance Publishing
IT Governance Limited
Unit 3, Clive Court
Bartholomew's Walk
Cambridgeshire Business Park
Ely
Cambridgeshire
CB7 4EH
United Kingdom

www.itgovernance.co.uk

First published in the United Kingdom in 2009
by IT Governance Publishing.

ISBN 978-1-905356-94-2

ABOUT THE SOFT SKILLS FOR IT PROFESSIONALS SERIES

IT is often seen as a 'hard-skill' profession where there is no place for soft skills. Yet the importance of soft skills for the IT professional should not be underrated; they underlie all behaviors and interactions. Both IT and non-IT professionals need to work together and learn from each other for effective business performance. All professionals, be they in IT or elsewhere, need to understand how their actions and reactions impact on their behavior and working relationships.

This series of books aims to provide practical guidance on a range of soft-skills areas for those in IT and also for others, including those who deal with IT professionals, in order to facilitate more effective and cooperative working practices.

Each book is written by an experienced consultant and trainer. Their approach throughout is essentially practical and direct, offering a wealth of tried and tested professional guidance. Each chapter contains focused questions to help the manager plan and steer their course. The language used is jargon-free, and a bibliography is included at the end of the book.

Angela Wilde

IT Governance

FOREWORD

Communication is to managing change as air is to breathing. Nobody knows this better than Naomi Karten. We who work at the intersection of business and IT are fortunate that she has written this book.

We first met Naomi Karten in 1989 in Mt. Crested Butte, Colorado. Coincidentally, our professional interest in human change started that same year, when we worked as IT managers for a large aerospace company. From then on, our paths kept crossing. Every September we would meet again in Mt. Crested Butte. In 1992, Wayne started teaching Problem Solving Leadership workshops with Naomi. In 1995, Naomi became Eileen's change consultant.

Here's how Eileen tells the story:

I was CIO for an insurance company. We had just been forced to merge our local data center into a megacenter, 700 miles away. Although the hardware move went well, production performance was a disaster. The users, managers, and finally my boss, the company president, were all calling me with complaints. After numerous polite requests to the megacenter director, I finally lost it one day on the phone with him. He responded in kind. Even though I considered myself pretty good at managing human change, I knew that I was heavily invested in this change and that it would be wise to look for unbiased external help. I yelled out to Naomi for help. She did a masterful job of helping the megacenter director and myself acknowledge our issues, express our expectations, negotiate our way through the chaos together, and rebuild the trust between us.

Naomi is a consummate professional who has 'been there, done that.' Her IT experience has spanned 15 years, working in industry as both individual contributor and manager. Layer onto that her 20 years as seminar leader and consultant to IT organizations and you have in Naomi a wise sage you can believe. If that weren't enough, her formal education in psychology and her extensive training in the methods of Virginia Satir, a pioneer in family systems therapy, add a special kind of credibility to her treatment of the human side of change.

Underneath her education and training, underneath her decades of IT experience, is an amazing woman with a huge heart and a great sense of humor. Naomi cares deeply that people struggle with change. Her caring and her humor come through in this book.

The advice in this book really works. We know it works because we use much of it in our consulting business. Our tag line is, 'Helping companies change how they change so they can do it faster, better, and easier.' We are hired by business executives to help them put troubled IT projects back on track. We most often find that failure to manage the human change is the biggest problem.

As heralds of change, you who work in and with IT will benefit from reading this book. You will better understand your own reactions to change and those of users, customers, employees, and suppliers. You will more confidently be able to explain why a one-size-fits-all change management plan doesn't work and how to make it more flexible. You'll understand more clearly why there is always a productivity drop when change is introduced and how to help people get up the learning curve more quickly.

This book is chock-full of useful models and tips that will increase your ability to deal with change more effectively, and help others do so as well. If you follow Naomi's advice in this book, your communication during a change process will be as healthy and invigorating as a breath of cool, clean mountain air.

Eileen Strider and Wayne Strider

Strider & Cline, Inc.

PREFACE

Have you ever driven on the other side of the road? I don't mean like in Boston, my hometown, where they do it for sport. I mean in a country where they drive on the opposite side of the road to what you're used to. It's an eye-opening experience when something as familiar as driving suddenly becomes unfamiliar.

That was my experience on a holiday in the UK with my husband, Howard. With confidence aforethought, he pulled right out into rush-hour traffic, as if he'd been doing other-side-of-the-road driving all his life.

For the first part of the day's outing, I served in a support capacity, which consisted of screeching, 'Keep left! Keep left!' This I interspersed with high-decibel shrieking when I thought a car coming toward us was going to smack into us. I shrieked a lot that day.

Then it was my turn to drive. 'Just keep left,' I told myself a few million times. After some initial shrieking – having excelled at it as the passenger, I kept it up as the driver – driving became more intuitive. Still, in focusing so intently on the left side of the road, we each veered too far left a few times, thereby grazing an assortment of immovable objects. And we went round and round in traffic circles, trying to summon the courage to exit.

The most striking part of the experience was how tiring it was. We were doing something that was totally familiar – driving – and yet so unfamiliar as to require intense concentration until new habits began to form. It reminded me of how mentally and emotionally demanding it can be to adjust to change. And how difficult it is not to make mistakes in learning new habits.

In the workplace, people on the receiving end of change often face uncertainty, self-doubt, confusion, and fear. At such times, what they need more than anything else is information, reassurance, encouragement, empathy, and feedback. Yet these are the very things that are most often lacking, as those in charge focus their attention on the technical aspects of the change and treat the people affected as an afterthought. And then they are puzzled when the people affected don't immediately welcome the change, support it, and adjust to it.

Your change efforts will proceed much more smoothly and to a much more satisfactory conclusion if you give serious consideration to the people affected. In fact, doing just that is the smartest way to minimize the duration and intensity of the turbulence that so often accompanies change.

With that in mind, my goal in writing this book is to offer ideas, guidelines, and advice to help you implement change in a way that respects the people affected. In particular, I want to help you excel at using communication as a tool for guiding people through change.

Having spent most of my career working in and with IT organizations, I've written this book for IT professionals and those who work with IT. These groups are my primary audience and the context for most of my examples and stories. But everything in the book applies to any line of work, even if it doesn't entail contact with IT.

And, of course, in addition to the never-ending changes at work, life is full of changes on the home front: marriage, divorce, illness, babies, children grown and leaving home (and these days, moving back), financial loss, and, of course, death of a loved one or pet. So, although the focus of this book is the workplace, everything I've written is relevant to your personal life as well.

In general, if you've ever experienced change in the past, or anticipate that you will in the future, this book is for you.

My approach to achieving my goal is:

1. To describe change efforts that backfired due to a failure to communicate and to suggest why communication is so often lacking during times of change. This is the focus of Chapter 1.
2. To present change models that offer insight into the experience of change. Chapters 2 and 3 describe these models.
3. To describe universal truths about the impact of change. This is what Chapter 4 addresses.
4. To highlight how people vary in their receptiveness to change and their response to it. Chapter 5 addresses these variations.
5. To guide you in reflecting on your own experiences in managing and coping with change. Chapter 6 offers self-assessment questions for this purpose.
6. To help you build a foundation that will support you when change arises. This is the subject of Chapter 7.
7. To offer suggestions for introducing change thoughtfully. Chapter 8 addresses this topic.
8. To provide guidelines for communicating to and with the people affected by change. This is the focus of Chapters 9 and 10.

9 To guide you in learning from your change experiences so that you become increasingly adept at managing and coping with change. Chapter 11 concludes the book with this topic.

Throughout the book, you'll find examples and more examples. Although it's probably not *your* workplace I'm describing in these examples, I predict that more than a few will sound familiar.

This book draws from my background in psychology, my technical and management experience in IT, and more than two decades serving IT organizations as a speaker, seminar leader, consultant, and author. I've worked in and with a vast number of IT organizations, as well as with the people who work with IT. I've seen a lot and learned a lot, and I'm happy to share it with you.

The great poet, Ogden Nash, master of humorous verses, once said, 'Progress is fine, but it's gone on long enough.' Who hasn't felt this way at times? I hope you find some ideas in this book that will help you to manage and cope with change successfully.

ABOUT THE AUTHOR

As a highly experienced professional speaker and seminar leader, Naomi Karten draws from her psychology and IT background to help organizations improve customer satisfaction, manage change, and strengthen teamwork. She has delivered seminars and presentations to more than a hundred thousand people in such diverse locations as Amsterdam, London, Oslo, Brussels, Vancouver, Toronto, Tokyo, Hong Kong, Trinidad, Costa Rica, San Francisco, Chicago, and New York.

Naomi's several service level agreement e-books, including *How to Establish Service Level Agreements*, have helped organizations worldwide establish successful SLAs. Her other books and e-books include *Managing Expectations*, *Communication Gaps and How to Close Them*, and *How to Survive, Excel and Advance as an Introvert*.

Naomi's website, www.nkarten.com, features more than a hundred articles on a wide range of topics, including strengthening customer relations, managing expectations, improving communication, gathering customer feedback, enhancing teamwork, and building consulting skills.

Naomi's newsletter, *Perceptions & Realities*, offers serious advice in a lively, chuckle-generating manner. Numerous issues of this newsletter are posted on her website. In addition, she has published more than 300 articles in print and online publications.

About the Author

Before forming her training and consulting business, Naomi earned degrees in psychology and gained extensive IT experience in technical, customer support, and management positions.

ACKNOWLEDGMENTS

Big hugs of appreciation to the following for your input, your stories and examples, your wisdom, your generous sharing of ideas, your offers of assistance, and your enthusiasm for the topic of this book. Thank you!

Szifra Birke
Fiona Charles
Dale Emery
Debbie Exner
Isabel Fenichel-Berg
Ellen Gottesdiener
Payson Hall
Sherry Heinz
Elisabeth Hendrickson
Pamela Livingston
Marco Riccioni
Lou Russell
Adrian Segar
Steve Smith
Eileen Strider
Wayne Strider
Becky Winant

Thank you also to Mark Tatro, Rotate Graphics, for cartoons that show the whimsical side of change.

CONTENTS

CHAPTER 1: COULD THIS BE YOU?

The residents of a small village reelected the dead mayor. According to one resident, 'I know he died, but I don't want change.'[1]

Whenever I mention this quote to people, they laugh. But often the laughter is accompanied by a nod of recognition. As amusing as this resident's comment is, the wish that things could be otherwise is a universal yearning. Who, after all, hasn't, at one time or another, wished that things could return to the way they once were?

People don't like change. Obviously, it would be inaccurate to claim that no one *ever* likes change. Life is one change after another. If we couldn't handle change, we couldn't survive. Most of the time, in fact, we just go with the flow and adjust slowly or quickly to each new thing that comes along. But changes that divert people from their chosen path can be unsettling, even frightening, and every one of us has experienced changes that threw us off balance.

The customers of IT organizations accept some changes readily and others less so; not surprising, perhaps, given the vast number of business, staffing, regulatory, workload, and other changes they contend with regularly. But it may be the changes driven by IT that pose the biggest challenge for these customers.

At a seminar I once conducted for an IT department and one of its customer departments, an IT project manager

---

[1] *Boston Globe*, 21 June 2008.

complained to the customers that they often took too long to respond to IT's needs. The customer manager's response: 'IT is 100% of what you do. It's *not* 100% of what *we* do. We have numerous responsibilities that have nothing to do with IT.' Several IT people looked stunned, as if they hadn't previously realized that their customers had any priorities other than the next IT-enabled change.

Surely, then, given IT's role as an agent of change, one might reasonably conclude that IT professionals accept change readily and with ease: new development methods, changes in hardware and software, new requirements, outsourcing, and all the rest. In my experience, however, and as I'll relate in this book, IT professionals are no less resistant to change than their customers – when it affects *them*.

So how do *you* respond to change when it's happening to *you*? And how do you handle change efforts that will affect your employees and colleagues, your customers (if you're in IT), or IT personnel (if you're one of its customers)?

To help you answer these questions, this chapter describes four change efforts – all true stories – that ran into serious problems because of a lack of consideration for the people affected. As you read these stories, think about whether anything similar has ever occurred in your own organization. The chapter then proposes some explanations for why helpful communication is so often lacking during change.

A case study of a painful change

This story illustrates what can happen when IT personnel fail to take company employees – their internal customers –

into account in implementing a major change. Sadly, it's just one of many situations I've encountered of a difficult change made worse by the failure to communicate.

An IT organization planned a company-wide desktop upgrade, one that entailed on-site adjustments to most of the company's desktop computers. The upgrade would be a considerable effort, but a worthwhile one that would benefit the company in cost savings, more reliable technology, and improved capabilities.

Glenn, the project manager of the upgrade implementation team, repeatedly asked his CIO, Russell, to send out a company-wide notice to alert everyone about the upgrade.[2] Russell refused. Trying to compensate for his CIO's failure to inform employees, Glenn notified department managers himself, but he lacked Russell's status and clout, and many managers ignored or dismissed his notice.

As a result, employees lacked an understanding of:

1 the reasons for the upgrade

2 how they would benefit

3 when the process would begin

4 how long it would take

5 who would carry out the upgrade

6 how departments could prepare

7 what would be different as a result of the upgrade

8 what they could do to minimize disruption to their work.

---

[2] The names of all individuals whom I describe by first name only have been changed, so that we can draw lessons from their experiences without embarrassing them.

What employees knew about the upgrade was basically nothing at all. Even managers knew almost nothing until Glenn contacted them to schedule the upgrades for their departments' computers. Still, such things don't remain secret for long. As soon as the upgrades began, the rumor mill went into action, circulating inaccurate information and distorting key details.

So, how did employees react to the upgrade? According to Glenn, they were furious, accusing him and his team of tampering with their computers and interfering with their work. They became even angrier – enraged in a few cases – when they had to cope with degraded system performance as the team resolved bugs and fine-tuned the network.

In addition, the help desk personnel, burdened with calls even during calmer times, were inundated. Their inability to keep up with questions and complaints exacerbated employees' anger.

Why, oh why, are customers so unhappy?

I help organizations manage customer expectations and improve customer satisfaction, and I learned about this fiasco when I was invited in – by Russell, no less, who wanted to know why his customers were so unhappy with

IT. Amazingly, he seemed clueless about IT's contribution to his customers' distress and dissatisfaction.

When I met with managers of several of the business units affected, I discovered that the experience was even worse than Glenn had portrayed it. Many of these employees didn't realize the upgrade was a company-wide effort, convinced instead that their department had been singled out for technology abuse. They saw the upgrade as being done *to* them, rather than *for* them; as being forced down their throats; as being foisted on them with no consideration for their priorities and obligations.

Having spent many years in IT and many more years as a consultant to IT organizations, I know how difficult these large-scale efforts can be. I was hoping to find something in the situation that would enable me to empathize with IT and come to its defense. But I was unable to do so. In this situation, IT blew it.

The outcome? The reputation of the implementation team was damaged. But more than just *their* reputation was hurt. Unable to distinguish one part of IT from another, business unit employees now viewed everyone in IT as a bunch of blundering, thoughtless tech-heads.

So, who suffered in this botched effort? The employees who used the upgraded computers, of course. But clearly Glenn, his team, the help desk, and all the rest of IT suffered too. Employees in many departments had previously had no contact with IT. Now, with this first exposure to IT, their impression was decidedly negative.

Although advance notification from Russell about the upgrade would have lessened the damage, Glenn and his team were guilty of focusing entirely on the technical issues while ignoring the human impact of the change.

Moral of the case study

Change is disruptive. Even if you do everything right, major change usually generates a good bit of grumbling and grousing from those on the receiving end. But ignoring the impact of a change on those who will be affected, sets the stage for an experience that will be far worse for them – and also for those implementing the change – than it might otherwise be. And a failure to communicate appropriately and adequately with those affected, both in advance of the effort and as it proceeds, is a major flaw in a great many change efforts.

Making matters worse, the negative aftereffects of a failure to communicate significantly outlast the duration of the event in which communication was lacking. And you can be certain that how you implement a change this time will affect how people respond to future changes. A reputation, once damaged, is tough to recover.

> How you implement a
> change this time
> will affect how people
> respond to future changes.

Three other painful experiences

Here, more briefly, are three other change efforts in which situations were made worse by a lack of consideration for the people affected, particularly in terms of communication.

Example 1: Just fill out the forms

Recognizing the need for a more rigorous approach to systems development, two IT directors introduced a new development methodology and sent IT personnel for training to learn how to use it. The training consisted of a sales pitch for the methodology, followed by a headache's worth of slides depicting the detailed, mind-numbing forms that either IT personnel or their customers would need to fill out in the course of a development project.

In addition to the training ... well, there was no 'in addition.' This so-called training was the extent of the preparation for this major change. Many developers quickly became loophole specialists, devising reasons why their project was an exception that could ignore the methodology or bypass some of its steps.

And IT's customers? Never mind training; they weren't even told that IT was implementing a new approach to development. Instead, customers started receiving forms from IT filled with questions they'd never before had to answer. Lacking an understanding of the questions, they simply left these sections blank. Use of the methodology remained lackadaisical for years, and systems continued to face delays and bugs that the methodology was intended to prevent.

Example 2: Spare them the distraction

Debbie, a marketing manager, was informed by her director that her department was going to be moved to another building where they would have more space than their current cramped quarters allowed. But she decided not to distract her staff with the news. They were facing demanding deadlines on several projects and she didn't want to add one more thing to their very full plates. Anyway, she knew they'd be pleased by their new quarters. With multiple meeting rooms, more work space, and better lighting, how could they not?

Working with the facilities department, Debbie took care of all the details of the move. Then, the Thursday before the move, she announced to her staff: 'Exciting news! Tomorrow is packing day. We're being moved to Building C over the weekend.'

Exciting news? Well, no, not really. The shock of Debbie's sudden announcement took a toll on productivity, not just while they unpacked and settled into their new space, but for weeks afterward. Even those who were pleased with the move were upset with Debbie for what one person described as 'her striking lack of the simple courtesy of telling us' about the move. Meaning, of course, in advance.

Debbie was a good manager. She cared about her staff. Unfortunately, her decision to withhold the news of the upcoming move made them suspicious of what else she might be keeping from them. Her good intentions led her team to distrust her. A sad situation.

Example 3: Just do your job

A national company, NatWideCo, was acquired by a large global company, GlobePlusCo, a situation that resulted in uncertainty, anxiety, and intense stress among NatWideCo employees. (These are fictional company names for real companies.) Although a reorganization of NatWideCo divisions was certain and layoffs were inevitable, months passed without any information from executives of either company. 'Just do your job' seemed to be their mantra.

But people who fear the worst don't function well. Rumors spread, feeding the fears and leading to a steady stream of NatWideCo employees quitting rather than waiting for they knew not what. The IT and finance divisions were especially hard hit, losing key people eager to bail out while they still had a chance of finding comparable positions elsewhere. Despite the obvious impact of these departures on both morale and productivity, NatWideCo officials behaved as if nothing was happening.

A manager, who was concerned about the serious toll the change was taking on NatWideCo employees, urged the company president to talk with employees. But he refused to acknowledge employees' concerns, or empathize with their fears – or even just let them know that this was a difficult time for one and all. And GlobePlusCo management did nothing to ease the situation.

The refusal of company officials to offer information, or even just to express concern for employees, resulted in a distrustful employee mindset that lasted for years and seriously prolonged the adjustment to the new company structure.

The failure to communicate – whether through refusal or shortsightedness, and whether innocently or deliberately – makes change efforts much more difficult than they need to be. Of course, communication alone is no guarantee of success and inappropriate, or ill-timed, communication can be every bit as damaging as none at all. But absence of communication that shows genuine concern for the people affected ensures that the effort will take longer, be plagued by more and bigger problems, and be far more painful than it might otherwise be.

Why communication falls short

Coming to terms with changed and changing circumstances entails adjustments of all kinds. People may need to adjust, for example, to a newly-scrambled organization chart, to new or departing team members, to the tools they're using, to the places and ways they do their work, and to the rules and regulations that guide them through the day.

But it's a mistake to confuse these external aspects of a change with the internal, gut-level, and sometimes gut-wrenching, *experience of change*. It's the experience of change that people in positions of leadership too often ignore – what people are going through in coping with and adapting to the change.

By people in positions of leadership, I don't mean just the people at the top. Rather, I mean anyone who works in or with IT and who directs, oversees, or influences the work of others. So I'm talking about team leaders, business analysts, project managers, department managers, senior managers, executives, and all others whose flawed communication can hinder or damage a change effort. For simplicity, I will henceforth refer to all such people simply as managers, unless I'm referring to a specific person in a position other than that of manager.

During the anxiety, uncertainty, and sometimes even shock triggered by major change, most people have an intense need to know what is happening and how it will affect them. Yet, strikingly often, communication in the form of information, feedback, reassurance, encouragement, and empathy is lacking. Managers function as though they hope that they'll be able to just slip the change in, and people won't notice the battering they're taking in the process. Maybe this time, people won't balk or resist or put up a fuss. Maybe this time, people won't wonder what they're not being told and will quietly go about their work. Maybe this time, people will rise up in unison and embrace the change. Such a reaction is not inconceivable. But only unwise managers count on it. All others recognize that caring communication is a critical tool for managing change successfully.

Why managers don't communicate

Not all managers are change-managing dunces, of course. Many managers excel at communicating with and showing concern for their employees, both during change and at all other times. Some do so intuitively. Some have had good role models, mentors, or coaches. Some have learned from experience, observation, training, or deep thought. Some gain ideas from books on the subject and other resources.

But what about the rest? In my work with organizations, I've found that the behaviors of most managers, who are guilty of flawed or inadequate communication during times of change, fall into categories that might be described as follows:

- **Obliviousness**. Many managers fail to appreciate the whack-in-the-head, punch-in-the-gut impact that change often has on those affected. People who fall into this category are often new to positions of leadership or otherwise inexperienced in leading others.

- **Cluelessness**. These managers have become so used to a constant state of change that they don't see the toll it takes on those less familiar with change, or more susceptible to it, than they are. As a result, they're blind to even the small steps they can take to help others cope with the change and adjust to it more readily.
- **Avoidance**. Even when managers understand the jolting impact of change, many avoid taking action because doing so means dealing with 'people issues' – feelings, in other words. Many of these managers are highly competent as technologists, but dealing with the messy people stuff is something they'd rather not do. So they don't.
- **Condescension**. These managers know what's good for everyone else and will decide whom to tell and when to tell whatever they decide is important enough to tell. Withholding information is their customary mode of operation.
- **Ignorance**. These managers know they ought to be doing something, but they don't know what, exactly. So they do their best. Unfortunately, sometimes their best does little to relieve the stress people are feeling during change. In some cases, doing their best actually makes things worse.

I used these designations – obliviousness, cluelessness, avoidance, condescension, ignorance – because they're the terms I often hear people use to describe such managers. And sure, there's some validity to these terms. But managing change is a challenging task, and most managers want to do a good job.

Accordingly, in the spirit of taking a hopeful approach to a difficult challenge, I propose a reframe of the above categories:

1 **Inexperience** (rather than obliviousness). Even though these managers have faced change as individual contributors, they are inexperienced in overseeing the work of others. Unlike more seasoned managers, they have enough to do just managing on a day-to-day basis; insight into how to help others cope with change is still foreign to them.
2 **Busyness** (rather than cluelessness). These managers are overwhelmed with responsibilities, many more than anyone else is aware of. They communicate all day, every day, but communication for purposes of reducing the turbulence of change just doesn't make it to their priority list.
3 **Discomfort** (rather than avoidance). Though their job descriptions may not say it in so many words, managers need to be part-psychologist. But managers aren't trained as psychologists. Dealing with behavioral issues, especially when emotions surface, is unnerving. Many managers are simply not comfortable in this realm.
4 **Caring** (rather than condescension). These managers are big-hearted people who care about their employees. Unfortunately, their compassion and concern lead them to feel protective, and so they withhold information, and especially bad news that employees would prefer to have.
5 **Lack of know-how** (rather than ignorance). For these managers, the issue is primarily an educational one. They need suggestions to help them apply their communication prowess during times of change.

So, what is it about change that those beset by inexperience, busyness, discomfort, caring, and lack of know-how need to know? Read on.

Food for thought

At the end of each chapter are a few questions that you might want to reflect on privately, or use as the basis for department or team discussions. In addition, some of these questions might serve as the basis for conversations between IT personnel and those who work with IT.

1 Have you ever observed a change effort similar to the any of the four described in this chapter? What were the circumstances? In your view, what was done well and what was missed?

2 Have you ever participated in a change effort similar to the any of the four described in this chapter? How did you view the effort at the time? How has your view of it changed (if at all) as a result of reading this chapter?

3 What do you take from this chapter that might lead you to manage change differently (or recommend that others do differently)?

4 Why do you think some managers don't communicate well during change? Consider the explanations in this chapter, or in any other, that make sense to you.

5 How well do *you* communicate during change? Would your customers agree (if you're in IT)? Would IT personnel agree (if you're a customer)?

CHAPTER 2: ILLUMINATING THE EXPERIENCE OF CHANGE

Think about a major change you experienced at work. How did it affect you? For example:

1 What was your initial reaction to the change?
2 Did you notice any impact on your concentration, mood, productivity, energy level, or health?
3 Did you at any point wish you could restore things to the way they were before?
4 What was the experience like in adjusting to the change?
5 How did your attitude and well-being after you adjusted to the change compare with when it first happened?

Numerous change models depict the experience that people have in accepting, absorbing, and adjusting to a change. This chapter begins with a glimpse of three models that *don't* reflect reality but nevertheless offer food for thought. It then presents the models of three individuals who deeply understand the experience of change: William Bridges, Elisabeth Kübler-Ross, and Virginia Satir.

Interestingly, the views of Bridges, Kübler-Ross, and Satir arose in very different contexts. Bridges devised his change model to address change in the workplace. Kübler-Ross's views on change came about in a hospital setting. Satir's arose in the context of family therapy. Although the work of these three individuals varies in emphasis and terminology, there is considerable overlap among them, and all three are relevant to understanding, managing and coping with change in organizational settings.

Models that don't reflect reality

Some change models don't hold up well once you think about them. In *Quality Software Management, Volume 4*, Gerald (Jerry) Weinberg describes several such models.[3] For example:

1. According to the Hole-in-the-Floor model, change is instantaneous and adjustment to the new performance level occurs immediately. This, of course, is not how change happens.
2. According to the Newtonian model, people can be induced or influenced to change through the application of appropriate rewards or threats. As Weinberg notes, this model introduces the human element, but its weakness is 'the totally inadequate model of humanity that's used; that people can be pushed around like billiard balls.'
3. According to the Learning Curve model, all change follows a learning curve: it takes time for people to respond to a change and adjust to it as the planners hoped. One limitation of the model, Weinberg points out, is that the learning curve represents an average picture of the learning of many individuals, often in a research setting, rather than the experience of real individuals in real organizations.

Almost all change models, including even these three, provide a focal point for reflecting on what contributes to, or detracts from, successful change efforts. But I hold an unfavorable view of models that view successful change

---

[3] Gerald Weinberg, *Quality Software Management, Vol. 4: Anticipating Change*, Dorset House Publishing, 1997, pp. 6–14.

management as primarily a matter of using the 'right' tools, software, techniques, and processes. Any change model that treats people as an afterthought, or that discounts or ignores how human beings really function, is flawed.

Contrast the views presented in these three flawed models with the views of Bridges, Kübler-Ross, and Satir. As described in the remainder of this chapter, each of these three individuals recognizes that change is much more than an objective, external event; change happens *to people*. All three understand that successful change requires attention to people and their needs. All three stress the role – and the power – of communication, as people come to terms with change.

William Bridges: Transitions

William Bridges is a business consultant and author of *Managing Transitions: Making the Most of Change.*

Bridges makes a distinction between change and transition, and this is a useful way to distinguish what we observe out there in the world from what we experience internally. Change, Bridges states, is situational. It refers to the person or thing that's new or different, such as new tools, new rules, a new project, a new location, a new process, or a new team leader.

Change, in other words, is external. What's internal – that is, what people experience – is transition, which he describes as the psychological process that people must go through to come to terms with the change.

Accordingly, Bridges describes the psychological response to change in terms of three stages:

1 **Ending**. This is the time during which you have to give up the familiar ways you are used to. In order to learn new ways, you have no choice but to put the old ways aside. This giving up or letting go – a necessary but difficult step – constitutes loss. Bridges encourages talking about the loss; he advises that not talking about a loss and pretending it doesn't exist is what causes problems.

2 **The neutral zone**. This is the uncomfortable, anxiety-provoking, and sometimes paralyzing time between giving up the old ways and accepting the new. Bridges describes the neutral zone as 'a nowhere between two somewheres.' It's often a time of tension, frustration, and ambiguity, but it also has a positive aspect, because its very neither-here-nor-there-ness makes it potentially a time of great creativity. As he states, 'The neutral zone is thus both a dangerous and an opportune place, and it is the very core of the transition process.'[4]

3 **Beginning**. This, according to Bridges, is what people both seek and want, but they may also find it unnerving when they are finally face to face with it because it means committing to the new way and doing things differently. Bridges emphasizes that beginnings are psychological phenomena; they are not simply a matter of carrying out specific tasks and activities. Beginnings take place only when people are 'ready to make the emotional commitment to do things the new way and see themselves as new people.'[5]

---

[4] William Bridges, *Managing Transitions*, Perseus Books, 1991, p. 6.
[5] Ibid., p. 50.

Normally, we think of human experiences as going from a beginning to an ending. But Bridges's terminology helps to emphasize that in terms of the psychological process of adapting to change, we begin with the ending – that which must be given up – and end with a new beginning.

Rarely is the journey from the ending to the new beginning easygoing and stress-free, and Bridges emphasizes the importance of communication during all three stages. For example, he advises that you:

1 Bring losses out into the open and acknowledge them, keeping in mind that loss is subjective and other people's experience of loss may differ from your own.
2 Give people information about what's happening. Putting it off to spare them from feeling upset can only generate bitterness and mistrust.
3 Provide communication channels that will minimize worrying and waiting.
4 Recognize that every policy, procedure, and list of priorities communicates a message.

Elisabeth Kübler-Ross: The five stages of grief

Elisabeth Kübler-Ross (1926–2004) was a Swiss-born and Swiss-educated medical doctor and psychiatrist who studied the stages people go through upon learning that they have a terminal illness. The five stages she identified are relevant not just to hospital patients facing death, but also to every one of us in our everyday lives. As described in her book *On Death and Dying*, the five stages are as follows:

1 **Denial**. This initial reaction to shocking news is usually a temporary defense or buffer. How quickly patients

emerge from denial depends on several things, including how much they are told about their condition and what they've learned through their life experiences about how to cope with stressful circumstances.

2 **Anger**. This is the stage patients move to when they can no longer remain in denial. In addition to anger, this stage can include a range of emotions, including rage, resentment, and envy. These emotions feed out in all directions, almost at random. This stage is understandably difficult for family members and others who care for the patient.

3 **Bargaining**. This stage represents hope. In this stage, patients bargain for a wish to be granted, as if asking, 'If I behave myself and do everything right, can I have just this one thing?' Not surprisingly, the wish is usually to be freed of the terminal situation or, barring that, a brief period without pain or discomfort.

4 **Depression**. This is the reaction that takes hold when denial, anger, and bargaining are replaced with a sense of loss, whether physical loss, financial loss, loss of family members or livelihood, loss of dignity, or loss of the ability to cope and have control over matters.

5 **Acceptance**. In this stage, patients are no longer angry or depressed about the impending outcome. Kübler-Ross points out that acceptance should not be misunderstood as a happy stage. But it is also not a time of resignation or hopelessness. Rather, this stage is a gradual acceptance of what is inevitable.

Kübler-Ross's book describes in detail the communication needs of terminally ill patients as they go through these five stages. Interestingly, the communication needs of people facing changes at work are strikingly similar. For example:

1 Patients knew about their condition, whether or not they had been explicitly told. The patient, Kübler-Ross says, will figure out what's really happening anyway, since most people aren't skilled enough actors to convey a cheerful demeanor over a long period. In the workplace, too, people sense what's going on even if they're not told. If they don't know the details, they invent them.

2 Many patients welcome someone who is willing to talk with them about their circumstances while still allowing them to maintain their defenses. In organizations also, many people facing change welcome the opportunity to talk about what they're experiencing.

3 Few people consider what is causing a patient's anger. Kübler-Ross recommends attempting to understand a patient's reactions rather than judging them, noting that patients who are treated with respect and understanding, and who are given time and attention, tend to lower their voices and make fewer angry demands. Might this not also be the case during change in the workplace?

4 Patients often did better if they felt they had some control over their situation, even if that control concerned only what they wanted to eat and when they were willing to have company. Indeed, in organizational settings, even a minimal sense of control can go a long way in easing the stress people feel.

5 Patients allowed to express sorrow over their condition often reach a state of acceptance more readily. Similarly, in organizations, managers who allow people to mourn

the loss of the old way and who show respect for this process can help them reach a state of acceptance more readily.

> Even a minimal sense of control can go a long way toward easing the stress people feel.

Of course, not everyone facing change goes through all five stages. An acquaintance of mine, upon learning of a serious medical diagnosis, leapt quickly from denial directly to acceptance; from 'oh no, not me' to 'let's take care of it.' He had no patience with the intervening stages, which he saw as unproductive. Still, most people in similar circumstances spend time in the middle stages.

Even if people go through all five of the stages, they don't necessarily do so in a straightforward fashion. Some people follow a different sequence, such as anger to depression to bargaining. Some repeat certain stages, such as anger to bargaining and back to anger. And, of course, people vary in how much time they spend at each stage and in the intensity with which they experience each stage – all these variations are perfectly normal.

In addition, people may go through other stages. When IT projects fail, some IT and customer departments spend an inordinate amount of time in a fault-finding stage. Of course, in some cases, this blaming behavior is a stalling tactic, since an objective assessment of contributors to the failure might point right back to the blamers.

Amusingly, Kübler-Ross's stages have inspired the use of similar stages for numerous life and business experiences. When I Googled 'five stages,' up came links to five stages of a business start-up, five stages of the collapse of a society, and five stages of dealing with new technology, among others. In a greetings card, I found the five stages of achievement: denial ('No way!'), indecision ('I should; no I shouldn't'), resistance ('My way is better'), panic ('Help, I'm stuck!') and acceptance ('Yay, I did it, time to party!').

Virginia Satir: an internal shift

Virginia Satir (1916–88) was a pioneer in the field of family therapy. At first glance, family therapy seems far removed from the business world. But Satir's concepts, models, and techniques have proven to be highly applicable in organizational settings. I am one of a growing number of organizational consultants who have studied Satir's ideas and methods in depth, and have found extraordinary acceptance of them among IT and business personnel.

Several of Satir's core beliefs relate directly or indirectly to the challenge of coping with change. For example:

1 The problem is not the problem; coping is the problem.

2 Most people choose familiarity over comfort, especially during times of stress.

3 Human processes are universal, and therefore occur in different settings, cultures, and circumstances.

4 We have choices, especially in terms of responding to stress instead of reacting to situations.

5 Change is possible. Even if external change is limited, internal change is possible.

6 We all have the internal resources to cope successfully and to grow.

7 We cannot change past events, only the effects they have on us.

> We cannot change past events, only the effects they have on us.
>
> *Virginia Satir*

An excellent resource on Satir's views on change is *The Satir Model* by Satir, John Banmen, Jane Gerber, and Maria Gomori. The authors describe change as 'basically an internal shift that in turn brings about external change.' They point out that this 'represents a major difference from approaches that work on changing from the exterior or on changing behavior only.'[6] Note that this matches Bridges's view that the adjustment to change is internal.

The Satir change model can help you understand not only how to implement and manage change, but also how to cope with it when you're on the receiving end. The model depicts the impact of change on an individual or group's performance or productivity and includes the following components:

1 old status quo
2 foreign element
3 chaos
4 transforming ideas
5 practice and integration
6 new status quo.

---

[6] Virginia Satir, John Banmen, Jane Gerber, and Maria Gomori, *The Satir Model*, Science and Behavior Books, Inc., 1991, p. 85.

This model has proven to be very appealing to people who manage or influence change in the workplace, or who are directly or indirectly affected by it. I've presented this model to a vast number of client organizations and professional groups, and people invariably connect with the wisdom it offers. I've also found this model valuable in helping me recognize my own reactions to change, enabling me to adjust to change more readily and with less stress and anxiety.

For these reasons, in the next several chapters I've chosen this model as the framework for a deeper discussion of how to treat people facing change.

Overlapping views of change

Clearly, there's considerable overlap among the views of Bridges, Kübler-Ross, and Satir. For example:

1 The term 'neutral zone' that Bridges uses for his middle stage may not provoke an image of turbulence, but don't be misled by his terminology. The neutral zone maps perfectly to Satir's stage of chaos.

2 A 'foreign element' (Satir's term) often triggers denial, the 'it can't be happening' reaction that Kübler-Ross described.

3 Kübler-Ross's middle stages of anger, bargaining, and depression may occur during Satir's stage of chaos and Bridges's neutral zone; for many people, these middle stages define the experience of chaos.

4 Acceptance, Kübler-Ross's final stage, is the result of emerging from chaos and achieving a new status quo.

You can undoubtedly identify many other ways in which these models overlap.

The next chapter describes the Satir change model in detail and explains its relevance to IT and those who work with IT.

Food for thought

1 Have you seen evidence in your organization of belief in the Hole-in-the-Floor model, the Newtonian model, or the Learning Curve model – the three change models described in this chapter that don't reflect reality? If you have, what was the impact of these beliefs?

2 What aspects of the views of Bridges, Kübler-Ross, and Satir appeal to you? What aspects would you refute?

3 Can you describe one or two ideas you got from this chapter that might influence your handling of future changes?

CHAPTER 3: CHAOS AND THE SATIR CHANGE MODEL

You can be more effective in coping with changes that come your way if you understand what makes change so unsettling and what you can do to expedite your progress to a new steady state. And you can be more effective in helping others cope with change if you understand what throws *them* out of balance and what you can do to help them restore a sense of balance.

This chapter presents the Satir change model as a framework for helping yourself and others through change.

The components of this model are:

1 Old status quo: the current normal.

2 Foreign element: the disrupting force.

3 Chaos: the reaction to a foreign element.

4 Transforming ideas: the way out of chaos.

5 Practice and integration: the adjustment to the change.

6 New status quo: the new normal.

The Satir change model

This model describes the impact of change on an individual or group's performance or productivity. How the model is presented visually varies with the preferences of the people who teach the model – I've seen probably a dozen different depictions of it. These various depictions include the same stages and use the same terminology, so if you read about this model elsewhere, you will find it familiar even if it looks different.

The depiction of the model in *Figure 1* is my own version of it, one that I like to use in my presentations because it's visual and colorful.

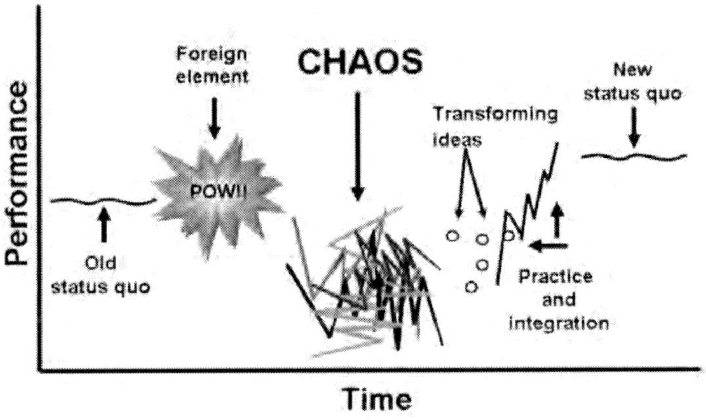

Figure 1: The Satir change model

Old status quo: the current normal

'Old status quo' refers to the way things are before a particular change comes along. Depending on the circumstances and the people involved, old status quo might be characterized by calmness, gentle ripples, roller-coaster-style ups and downs, or anything in between. Once a change disrupts things, people often look back at the old status quo as the good old days, when things were so much better, at least in retrospect.

I often use the phrase *current normal* to describe this stage. During the turbulence of change, people sometimes wonder if things will ever return to normal. And usually they will, but to a new normal. So I use *current normal* to contrast with the *new normal* and to emphasize that the current state of things may not last indefinitely. However things are today, they might be very different tomorrow.

Foreign element: the disrupting force

This is Satir's term for something that happens to upset the status quo and throw the system into chaos. A foreign element can be an event, an announcement, a situation, a surprise, a realization, a thought, a remark, a rumor, or anything else that disturbs the relative balance, comfort, and familiarity of how things have been.

Figure 2: How a foreign element often feels

Figure 2 shows how I think of foreign elements, because it's how they often feel.

What kinds of things have been foreign elements in your workplace? When I've asked people who work in or consult to IT organizations to identify a foreign element they've observed or experienced, they've overflowed with examples, including these:

1 Reorganizations, layoffs, cutbacks, outsourcing.
2 A new boss or supervisor.
3 New rules, processes, or guidelines.
4 The addition or termination of key personnel.
5 Major changes in the mission of the organization.
6 Technological change that affects the way people do their jobs.
7 Financial crisis or major shifts in the economy.
8 A move to a new home or work location.
9 Conflicting information from suppliers.
10 Personal events that affect the ability to do the job.
11 A sudden change in priorities.
12 An outage affecting a large geographic area.
13 A technology upgrade.
14 An abruptly cancelled project.
15 The transition to agile methods for software development.
16 The requirement to begin pair programming.
17 A promotion.
18 Rumors of drastic but unspecified changes.
19 The discovery of bugs that will delay implementation.
20 New requirements from third parties.

Some of the examples in this list are IT-specific, but when I've asked IT's customers to identify their own examples of foreign elements, their responses have been very similar.

Indeed, whether you are in IT or you work with IT, similar things can upset the status quo.

The preceding foreign elements can have a major impact, especially if several of them strike in close proximity. But even transient situations at work can be foreign elements, such as:

1 Your laptop computer getting stolen from your car.
2 A bizarre error message when you're on a tight deadline.
3 The first day (or week or month) on a new job.
4 A voicemail message from your boss's boss to 'see me immediately.'
5 Going blank during a crucial presentation.
6 Disruption of your e-mail service.
7 Cancellation of a flight to an important event.
8 Your computer freezing during a demo to the CEO.
9 Your computer unfreezing – and then going haywire.
10 Realizing that you've forgotten an important meeting.
11 Accidentally hitting 'send all' for a message best kept private.

Uncertainty itself can be a foreign element. Should we outsource with this vendor or that one? Did we make a mistake in hiring that analyst? Will I get in trouble for my snide remark when the customer asked for just one more change?

Rest assured that executives are not immune to foreign elements. Eileen Strider, a consultant to senior executives, told me of a situation in which senior executives opted out of reviewing a new process before the design phase was completed. Alas, they were too busy. But, as Strider reports,

They hit the roof after go-live when they realized their approval was no longer required to add staff to their departments. Their administrative staff person could simply key in the new employee data, and the employee was entered into the HR system with no review or approval.[7]

Surprise!

Of course, our personal lives are also packed with foreign elements, including those with a significant or tragic impact such as divorce, death of a loved one, loss of a job, an injury, financial crisis, or a natural disaster. But even relatively inconsequential foreign elements can jangle your nerves, such as:

1 Hearing the phone ring in the middle of the night.
2 Having your car break down on a busy motorway.
3 Dropping your keys onto the railway tracks.
4 Kicking a sofa leg in anger and feeling the pain.
5 Hearing a police siren right behind your car.
6 Having your youngster spill glue on your keyboard.
7 Your in-laws coming to visit – for three months.
8 The many differences you encounter when traveling abroad.

As these examples illustrate, a foreign element can be:

1 big or small
2 brief or prolonged
3 expected or unexpected
4 planned or unplanned

---

[7] I conducted numerous interviews for this book. This story and many of the other stories and examples that you'll read about came out of these interviews.

5 the presence of something unfamiliar
6 the absence of something familiar.

We experience foreign elements differently

No one thing is necessarily a foreign element for everyone. Whether something affects any given individual as a foreign element depends on numerous factors, such as past experience, inner resources, competing priorities and likely, or imagined, consequences.

In addition, a foreign element can be positive for some people and negative for others, or positive at one point in time and negative at another. For example, a project manager might view the unexpected transfer to another team as positive if it occurs after the completion of the current project, but negative if it occurs in the middle of the current project.

Note also that a change that takes effect over time, such as a merger or a natural disaster, can present a succession of foreign elements. Indeed, life is pretty much one foreign element after another: some expected, others unexpected; some big, many small; some transient, others long term.

A comment about terminology

'Foreign element' was Satir's term, and I use it in this book out of respect for her work. But I've learned that some people dislike the term, asserting that it sounds like it refers to someone from another country or culture – a foreigner, in other words, and one who may not be altogether desirable.

This is a valid concern, and I've considered alternatives that would convey the intended meaning of 'foreign element.' Most of the terms I've considered fall short. For example:

1 *Surprise* isn't good because some foreign elements can be anticipated. It's not a surprise when a new CEO takes over after the previous one left – although the CEO's actions upon taking over may prove to be a surprise.
2 *Shock* can be too strong. I heard about a department in which the coffee pot was moved to another spot in the office, and for weeks afterwards people complained about the additional steps they had to take to get their caffeine fix. Foreign element though this change may have been, it doesn't qualify as a shock (caffeine addicts may disagree).
3 *Interference and disturbance* don't work because they suggest that a foreign element is negative, and that's not necessarily the case. My friend Ravi, who became a manager after aspiring to the position for years, described his promotion as a very happy foreign element.

The term I like most as an alterative to foreign element is *jolt*. The website <u>*www.answers.com*</u> provides this definition (among others):

Jolt: something that jars the mind or emotions.

This definition aptly captures how we experience foreign elements; indeed, they can throw both one's mind and one's emotions off kilter.

If you will be presenting this model to your own colleagues and prefer not to use the term 'foreign element,' simply select an alternative term of your own choosing. If you do, I suggest you at least mention the term 'foreign element,' since it's the term people will encounter if they read about the model.

Chaos: the reaction to a foreign element

Chaos can occur in everyday experiences, such as during a rapid-fire brainstorming session, or when you watch in horror as, with only minutes remaining, your favorite sports team fumbles. And what about remodeling your kitchen? Anyone who has undertaken a renovation that disrupts the normal flow and is plagued by delays and problems knows about chaos. In fact, some contractors give customers a copy of their own version of the change cycle to prepare them for the undertaking.

In the Satir model, 'chaos' is a technical term that describes a state of turbulence triggered by a foreign element that affects one's mental, physical, and emotional well-being.

When a foreign element throws an individual or group into this state of turbulence, the result is an out-of-balance condition in which productivity is temporarily impaired. Turbulence is a state that may entail commotion, confusion, turmoil, disorder, unrest, instability, uproar (all synonyms for turbulence) – as well as disarray, bedlam, upheaval, pandemonium, and disruption (synonyms of the synonyms).

Who knew there were so many words that capture the turbulence triggered by change? And one of the definitions for 'chaos' offered by *www.answers.com*, which provided me with the definition for jolt, is 'utter confusion.' Exactly!

Figure 3 captures my own view of how chaos looks and feels.

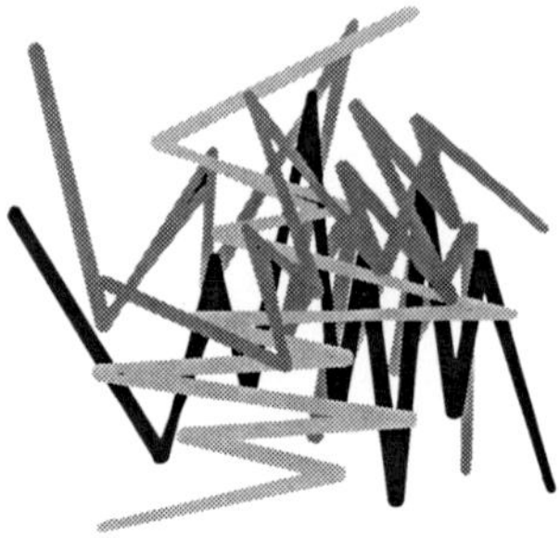

Figure 3: How chaos looks and feels

What's important to understand is that chaos is normal. The chaos you feel when confronted with a foreign element is perfectly normal. And the chaos that others feel is perfectly normal. Chaos is real and it plays out over time. No one who experiences a foreign element is immune. But how you communicate can reduce – or exacerbate – the duration and intensity of that chaos.

What's important to understand is that chaos is normal.

Chaos is characterized by stress and unease. But it can be much worse than that. While in chaos, people might feel like they've been whacked in the head, punched in the stomach, or bounced from a bungee cord. They might become preoccupied, absent-minded, forgetful, confused, distracted, or fatigued. Their sense of time might become distorted. They might have difficulty concentrating on their work. Needless to say, all these reactions are likely to reduce productivity and increase mistakes.

In addition, people in chaos might experience physical symptoms, such as an upset stomach, headache, or backache. Of course, these symptoms are not necessarily a sign of chaos; a stomachache might just be the consequence of that extra slice of pizza for lunch. But physical symptoms are not unusual during chaos.

People might also react with shock, anxiety, fear, or anger. In fact, at the height of chaos, people often experience a flood of emotions, almost an assault of emotional reactions that are neither expected nor wanted – but there they are. Note that these reactions are possible even when the chaos is triggered by something positive – win the jackpot in the lottery and you'll see!

These mental, physical, and emotional reactions are often accompanied by changes in behavior. When in chaos, people might whine, complain, fuss, protest, or nitpick more than usual – or become quieter than usual. Your behavior while in chaos might (once you're clearheaded again) lead you to think, 'That wasn't like me at all.' In fact, if you notice a change in others from their normal behavior, it could be a sign that they're in a state of chaos.

Given the potent impact of chaos, it's both pointless and unproductive to expect people to adjust immediately to a given change. In fact, unduly coaxing them to 'get on with it, already,' might just prolong and intensify their chaos. Obviously, this is not to say that work must stop until everyone has adjusted – imagine an IT or business project that can be placed on hold whenever there's a foreign element – but it does mean that the impact of chaos must not be overlooked.

A different kind of chaos

In November 2001, two months after the 11 September attacks, I was scheduled to give a presentation at a bank just a few blocks from the wreckage of the World Trade Center. Coincidentally, my topic was 'Changing How You Manage Change' and I was planning on presenting the Satir change model.

Big cities like New York are busy, energetic, fast-paced places. But on 11 September, things changed. In the days and weeks that followed, the pace slowed. Interactions became characterized by gentleness, concern and compassion. Driven by a shared tragedy, strangers and friends alike showed sensitivity to each other's feelings. People who might otherwise have taken offense at some perceived misdeed reacted with kindness.

When I gave my presentation, many people voiced hope that this caring behavior would become the norm. But such was not to be. Using the Satir change model, I explained that this gentleness and sensitivity were not signs of a new status quo, but rather symptoms of the chaos people were experiencing. I further explained that we would know that the city was emerging from chaos when the pace picked up, people were again rushing about, and some of the abruptness resumed.

It took time, but in terms of the way people interacted, the city eventually returned to its former self.

An often overlooked source of chaos

When I ask audiences to identify things they have found to be foreign elements, they cite the sorts of events, news, and announcements that I described in the previous lists. But there's one other very important foreign element and it's often missing from their examples. *Figure 4* describes that foreign element.

Figure 4: The source of many foreign elements

What this means is that if it is your responsibility to introduce or implement change – or even just to know the status of a change – those who are affected by the change may experience *you* as a foreign element and therefore the trigger that throws them into chaos.

Indeed, those whose very job it is to be of service are often the biggest sources of chaos.

By their very nature, the roles played by IT professionals often create chaos for their customers – and conversely, the roles played by IT's customers often create chaos for IT. And those who work in and with IT can create chaos for their own coworkers and colleagues.

In particular, you may provoke chaos in others in the way that you

1 offer ideas

2 present bad news

3 introduce new options

4 try to change people's minds

5 say no (not now, not this way).

So, for example, if an IT team waits until the last minute to notify customers that a project they're involved with is slipping – or customers wait until the last minute to notify IT that they can't meet agreed deadlines – the ultimate confession of a delay may propel the other party into chaos. If you're in IT and you use an aggressive tone to suggest that customers defer certain functions until the next release, you might drive them into chaos. And if you're a customer and you demand that an IT team incorporate changes that you had agreed to defer until the next release, you might drive the team into chaos.

If you tell another party, 'Sure, we can do it' (whatever 'it' is) when you're not so sure, and you tell them, 'Sorry, we can't,' only when it's too late for them to plan alternatives, don't be surprised if you force them into chaos.

In each of these examples, and others than you can identify from your own activities, you may be a foreign element that shoves others into a state of chaos. Therefore, the way you communicate with them may have a significant bearing on the way they respond to you and to the change you are introducing.

The remainder of this book provides advice on how to communicate to minimize any such chaos. For now, here is what is most important in terms of communication:

> What, when and how you communicate
> with those who are affected by a given change
> influences the *duration* and the *intensity*
> of the chaos they experience.

In other words, the things you say or do (or neglect to say or do) during times of change can exacerbate the duration and intensity of the chaos people experience – or reduce it, helping them to move expeditiously and productively toward a new status quo.

Transforming ideas: the way out of chaos

Transforming ideas are ideas that people in chaos get consciously or subconsciously that help them move into a stage of practice and integration on the way to a new status quo.

Transforming ideas that I've seen help people emerge from chaos include these:

1 The willingness to accept sources of support previously rejected.
2 The willingness and courage to try new approaches.
3 The discovery of alternative solutions that might work.
4 The discovery of different ways to solve a problem.
5 The realization that the solution they're looking for is right in front of them.
6 The realization that things won't turn out as badly as previously imagined.
7 Looking at the change from a different perspective and seeing a happier outcome.
8 Acceptance of benefits not previously appreciated.

Transforming ideas help those affected by a change to realize that they will survive the change and maybe even benefit from it.

For example, as Sheila, a project manager, struggled with the aftermath of a difficult reorganization, her new manager invited her to participate in a complex project. From his description, the project didn't pique her interest and she felt inclined to turn it down. Plus, she wasn't too impressed with this manager, whom she didn't think she could work well with or learn from. After much deliberation and encouragement from friends, she decided to give it a try. If it didn't work out, she concluded, she'd find a way out.

The manager proved to be an excellent coach and mentor. And the project was a turning point in her career, leading her into positions and opportunities that might never have come her way if she had rejected the transforming idea of giving it a try.

Sources of transforming ideas

The most common source of transforming ideas is simply the passage of time, because time allows stress to diminish and clarity to surface. Specific activities that can also help transforming ideas to surface include:

1 talking with friends or colleagues

2 asking for help

3 attending a class

4 taking a break

5 getting some exercise

6 doing some brainstorming

7 taking a nap (or several)

8 doing research

9 meditating

10 explaining your problem to someone unfamiliar with it

11 explaining your problem to your child

12 couch-potatoing

13 reading related or unrelated books.

One of the best ways to get transforming ideas is to change your perspective – either mentally, by thinking about the situation from a different angle; or physically, by getting up and moving elsewhere. Many programmers can recall a time when they were stymied by a coding problem, and as soon as they approached a coworker to ask for help, the solution came to them.

A transforming idea is worthless, though, if people reject it or fail to notice it. In a simulation I sometimes use in my experiential workshops, software engineers work in teams to solve a complex problem within a strict time limit, a situation that quickly thrusts them into chaos. Clues – transforming ideas – that would help them solve the problem are posted on classroom walls and included in their written instructions.

But people in chaos sometimes become so focused on the immediate situation that they're blind to what's going on around them. In running one of these simulations, I gave a participant a yellow sheet of paper that offered a key clue. In no time, the sheet became buried under other material the group was working with. He never even looked at it. In successive offerings of this simulation, people rarely noticed the clues.

A key in moving to a new status quo is being open to the presence of transforming ideas. Therefore, try not to hastily reject ideas offered by others because 'we tried that last year and it didn't help,' or because you're convinced it's the wrong solution. Remaining open to the potential for transforming ideas in the ideas and suggestions of others often expedites the journey to a new status quo.

Practice and integration: the adjustment to the change

This stage refers to the effort needed to integrate new knowledge and skills. Moving out of chaos and into a new status quo entails learning, practice, experience, reflection, and the formation of new habits.

Some change models omit this stage, viewing the individual or group as going from chaos (or the model's equivalent) directly to the new normal. Other models acknowledge this adjustment process but don't cite it as a distinct stage. Its explicit inclusion is one of the strengths of the Satir model.

Some people refer to this stage as 'integration and practice.' In their view, people first integrate the components of the change and then learn through practice how to put it all together so that it's natural and familiar. From my own perspective, it's through practice that we become able to integrate the components of the change, so I prefer to call this stage 'practice and integration.'

Whichever version you prefer, it's certain at this stage that people won't get everything right the first time around, and maybe not the second or third time, either. As they tackle new methods, procedures, rules, or ways of functioning, they will inevitably make mistakes. They may fumble and stumble and take longer than they would if they were already proficient in the matter. They may even slip back into chaos, where they thrash around for a while, before returning to practice and integration.

If you're leading a change effort, don't expect too much of people too soon. Instead, acknowledge their progress, be supportive of their new learning, provide handholding if needed, and be as patient as you can with the likely decrease in productivity.

New status quo: the new normal

In the model, if not always in real life, the individual, group, or organization eventually regains its equilibrium.

Sometimes those who are affected by a change are happier or more productive in the new status quo than they were before the change. Sometimes, they're not. But by going through the change cycle, they may have gained wisdom about coping with change that will enable them to handle other changes more capably in the future.

The trip through the change cycle

Although the Satir model depicts the stages of change as occurring in a systematic, sequential fashion, the journey to a new status quo may be less orderly than that. For example, in trying to repel the foreign element, a team may retreat to the old status quo and hang on tight. An individual or team may be on the verge of achieving a new status quo, and slip back into practice and integration, or even chaos. Some people may reach a new status quo before others. Every change has an itinerary of its own.

Food for thought

1 What kinds of things are foreign elements for you? What kinds of things seem to be foreign elements for your coworkers? Do you and your coworkers react to the same things or different things as foreign elements?

2 Think of change efforts you've observed or experienced that triggered chaos. What was chaos like for you? For others? How did people behave while in chaos?

3 In these change efforts, how would you describe the communication that took place or failed to take place? What impact did it have on the duration and intensity of the chaos?

4 In terms of the Satir change model, what do you see as opportunities for improvement in future change efforts?

CHAPTER 4: UNIVERSAL TRUTHS ABOUT CHANGE

Change would be so much easier to cope with if only we could make our way from old status quo, through chaos, to new status quo, uninterrupted by other chaos-producing circumstances. And wouldn't it be refreshing if, having reached a new status quo, we could relax there for a while before facing the next bout of chaos?

But life is a series of foreign elements that come at us from all directions. Invariably, whether we're luxuriating in old status quo, coping with chaos, traversing practice and integration, or settling into a new status quo, there's another foreign element and another and another.

The amazing thing, really, is that most people function reasonably well most of the time, despite so much chaos.

Drawing from the models described in the previous two chapters, this chapter takes a look at nine truths about the experience of change that will deepen your understanding of change and your ability to manage it and cope with it:

1 Significant change is a felt experience.
2 People believe they are immune to chaos.
3 Resistance is a common response to a foreign element.
4 All change involves loss.
5 Recurring situations affect chaos differently.
6 Irreversible decisions made when in chaos are risky.
7 Significant change entails a drop in productivity.
8 Learning entails chaos, and chaos triggers learning.

9 Practice and integration is a time of ups and downs.

Significant change is a felt experience

Significant change can be viewed as change that packs a wallop. Given this powerful impact, people's responses to it are likely to be emotional and visceral rather than logical and rational.

Therefore, if you communicate with people in chaos in a logical and rational manner, they may not be able to absorb your message. Worse, they may resent what they perceive as your inability or refusal to appreciate what they're going through. Research into brain functioning bears this out: our brains function differently when we're in an emotional state than when we're calm and rational.

> People's responses to significant change are likely to be emotional and visceral rather than logical and rational.

Don't take the misguided approach proudly described by a project leader, Stan, when I presented the Satir model in his organization. Stan explained that when he noticed a former coworker, Tracy, showing signs of chaos triggered by a foreign element in her personal life, he told her, 'You're in chaos now. But don't worry. It's normal. It'll pass. You'll get over it.' He thought he was doing the right thing in educating Tracy about chaos while she was *in* chaos. He was wrong.

The printable portion of Tracy's response was, 'Get lost.' The rest I leave to your imagination. Speaking to someone in chaos in a patronizing, know-it-all manner is not likely to diminish their chaos. At such times, caring communication that focuses on empathy, acknowledgment and a healthy dose of listening is far more considerate. Stan might have acknowledged Tracy's situation by saying, 'I'm sorry to hear what you're going through.' If he felt it appropriate, he might have offered a helping hand to ease her workload. Or he could simply have said, 'If there's anything I can do to help, let me know.'

People believe they are immune to chaos

Actually, educating people about chaos isn't necessarily easy even when they're clearheaded. 'No big deal,' they think. 'I can handle it.' But can they? In *The Change Monster*, Jeanie Duck describes the experience of a consulting colleague who tried to prepare a CEO client for the chaos that would arise during an upcoming merger.

The colleague forewarned his client that the change would be accompanied by extreme emotional ups and downs among employees from both companies. People who had been reliable and self-confident would face anxiety and doubt. Loyal people would become disloyal. Trusted advisors would start clinging to their turf. At the same time, others who had never risen to a challenge before would go above and beyond.

The important thing, the consultant explained, was to expect the unexpected, not just from employees, but also from all sorts of progress-inhibiting problems, from natural disasters to customer uprisings. And finally, the consultant pointed out, the CEO himself would be severely tested and would require extraordinary levels of energy and determination to make the merger work.

As Jeanie Duck describes it, 'The CEO, a seasoned and internally respected executive, listened patiently to my colleague and then, when he had finished, remarked with more than a hint of condescension, "I think we can handle it."'[8]

Any guesses about what happened?

The consultant's predictions proved to be on target in even more serious ways than he'd anticipated. As the merger proceeded, an executive from the acquiring company, laid off from a position he had believed to be permanent, committed suicide. The CEO, badly shaken, accused the consultant, claiming he had never said it could get this bad.

Rest assured that this is an extreme example; suicide is not normally on the list of things you need to worry about during times of chaos. But this story superbly exemplifies how quickly people who have been 'warned' about the turbulence of change can dismiss it if they haven't previously experienced it.

Resistance is a common response to a foreign element

People who deny a given change, or cling to the ways of the old status quo, often display such behaviors as excuses, complaining, procrastination, and confrontation. Such people are frequently described as being 'resistant to change.'

The tendency to persist in doing things the old way has existed throughout the history of computer technology. For example, when English-like query, analysis, and reporting

---

[8] Jeanie Daniel Duck, *The Change Monster*, Three Rivers Press, 2001, p. xiv.

languages came along, many programmers came up with one excuse after another for why they didn't want to use these languages. When they finally attempted to write programs using these languages, they struggled because they kept trying to apply the logic and syntax of the more complex languages they already knew.

Meanwhile, their customers, lacking technical expertise, readily learned these languages, an intolerable situation to the struggling programmers. I recall people from human resources, payroll, legal, and benefits administration departments who chuckled with glee at being able to use these languages to do their own queries and generate their own reports.

Many software engineers are now facing similar struggles in companies that are adopting agile methods of software development. Ellen Gottesdiener, an expert in requirements identification and author of *Requirements by Collaboration*, has observed technical personnel anxiously struggling to adapt to a methodology in which they could ease up on the up-front requirements effort. Their tendency is to keep going back to their old tool to record each change.

Dale Emery, a consultant and deep thinker on resistance, points out that dealing with resistance can be tricky because people sometimes don't want to explain their real reasons for not wanting to go along with a given change. Instead, they often give a socially acceptable explanation, such as 'I don't have the time' – the most common explanation – or 'I'm busy,' a close second.

The starting point in dealing with resistance is often a terminology adjustment. If your tendency is to label people as resistant to change, Emery urges that instead you think of them as people who are resisting this change at this time.

This seemingly small adjustment is significant because it acknowledges them as human beings who have reasons for resisting. Emery also recommends that instead of thinking of people as resisting a change, you think of them as responding to it.

This is much more than just fiddling with words. These terminology adjustments promote a mindset that supports talking with people, listening carefully to their concerns, acknowledging the validity of these concerns, and finding ways to address them. In general, watch your language and your attitude as you urge people to accept a change. As Emery notes, the harder you push for people to get on with it, 'the more likely their resistance is not to what you are pushing for, but to your pushing so hard without regard for their interests.'[9]

Resistance to change is a normal human response. It's normal for people to want to stay where things are familiar. Rather than be surprised, wise managers anticipate these reactions. There may be no reason for concern unless these behaviors are excessive, disruptive or prolonged.

Keep in mind that sometimes resistance serves a positive end. Farmers seek varieties of crops that can resist infestation by insects or outbreaks of disease. And in organizations, the people who 'resist' are sometimes the ones most worth listening to because they have legitimate concerns that others are overlooking in their eagerness to move forward.

---

[9] Dale Emery, *Resistance as a Resource*, unpublished, p. 54. See *www.dhemery.com/articles* for some of Emery's published writings on resistance.

All change involves loss

We tend to view change in terms of *changing to* rather than *changing from*. But it's the *changing from* that often poses the biggest challenge. In *Managing in Times of Change*, Michael Maginn refers to change as the 'from–to,' going *from* the ways things are now *to* something different.

Maginn advises that a critical component of managing change is analyzing what the from–to will be for the people affected. This analysis entails assessing such things as the changes in staffing numbers, the tools and resources to be gained or lost, the work that will demand more or less time and effort than before, the standards and processes that will change, and the measures that are different and perhaps unfamiliar.

Maginn emphasizes that managers who understand the from–to will be in a better position to explain it to their teams. He especially encourages managers to identify the big impacts, noting that every change 'usually has at least one – usually more – major implications for how things operate. Locate what those are.'[10]

In general, coping with change entails coming to terms with loss, and grieving is a common way of coping with loss. Fiona Charles, a software-testing consultant, notes, 'People can become deeply attached to an organization, a job, or a role where they feel important or needed, and mourn their loss very keenly. Sometimes, forced to retire from a fulfilling job, they even die.'

---

[10] Michael D. Maginn, *Managing in Times of Change*, McGraw-Hill, 2005, p. 4.

Coping with change entails coming to terms with loss.

Grieving is a process usually associated with the death of a loved one. But grieving is just as relevant in losses in the workplace, such as the loss of security, of a sense of belonging, of daily patterns, of communication channels, and of friends who are terminated. Giving up almost anything people cherish is a form of loss, and that's the case whether it was taken away or given up voluntarily. In all these instances, people may need to grieve.

The English language does a poor job of distinguishing different kinds of loss. Other languages, including some arcane ones, do better. For example, in reading *The Writing on the Wall* by Lynne Sharon Schwartz, I learned that the language of Etinoi (a South Seas Island language) has separate words for different varieties of loss:

1 Loss of a person by death, as we mean it in English.
2 Loss of a small object, such as by being misplaced.
3 Loss of a large object, such as by theft or destruction.
4 Loss of a situation or a way of life, such as your job or location.
5 Loss of a state of mind or state of being, such as loss of security, success, or happiness.[11]

Furthermore, each of these distinct words for 'loss' can be modified by a choice of suffixes that indicate whether the thing lost can be regained – such as by finding the lost

[11] Lynne Sharon Schwartz, *The Writing on the Wall*, Counterpoint, 2005, pp. 43–4.

object or regaining the success – or whether it's lost for good, as in the case of death or destruction.

In English, alas, we have but the single word, 'loss.' But what's important in the context of change is recognizing that, for many people, the process of giving something up is a loss and coping with that loss can take a toll. Clearly, therefore, it's a mistake to ignore, discount, or trivialize the loss. And it's a mistake to focus entirely on what's being changed while ignoring the people affected by the change.

Even good news, such as a promotion or new job, entails loss. Such changes require the loss of familiar ways of doing work, and the relationships and reputation associated with the previous position.

As stated by a character in Jeanne Ray's delightful novel, *Eat Cake*, upon recognizing that some long-awaited good news would necessitate loss: 'I never knew that people could be afraid of good news too. I realized that good news took you places you didn't know anything about. It changed everything as much as bad news did.'[12]

Recurring situations affect chaos differently

In certain situations, it's not the first occurrence of a foreign element that causes chaos, but its repetition. In observing changes in reporting structure, company vision, methodologies, and processes, Sherry Heinze, a test strategist, has found that people are often not overwhelmed the first time through; it's the recurrence that causes chaos and serious problems.

---

[12] Jeanne Ray, *Eat Cake*, Shaye Areheart Books, 2003, p. 201.

In other cases, recurring situations lose their power to create the same level of chaos. A business analyst I know described the succession of managers his department had had. 'We're on our fifth manager in three years,' he told me. The first change in managers threw the staff into chaos; thereafter, the very fact of management changes became the staff's old status quo.

As a professional speaker, I've faced no end of foreign elements. I well remember the time the program director brought the screen to the off-site meeting, but forgot the projector; the time the material I'd shipped was sent to a town of the same name 2,000 miles away; and the time my presentation was accompanied by the sound of a high-decibel whackety-whackety-whack from the construction work going on right outside.

I used to feel certain that, eventually, I'd have experienced everything that could possibly go wrong; but no, even after 20 years as a professional speaker, foreign elements still enliven my speaking engagements. Now, instead of being thrown into chaos, I remain calm and view the experience as a story for a future presentation. Usually.

Irreversible decisions made when in chaos are risky

One of the challenges chaos poses is recognizing you're in it when you're in it. Unfortunately, it's difficult to recognize that you're in chaos because you're *in it*. The real maturity in coping with chaos is being able to recognize a foreign element when it strikes and to say to yourself, 'I'm in chaos and I feel miserable. But I will survive. Now what do I need to do for myself, so I can get out of chaos as fast as possible and find my way to a new status quo?'

This is important: do your best not make *any* important, irreversible decisions when you're in chaos, or you may regret it later on. When you're in chaos, it's natural to want to do something – *anything* – to fix the situation, ease the pain, or escape its discomfort. The temptation can be overwhelming to quit your job, scream at your customer, take a bat to your computer, or buy something you can't afford.

But when your thought processes are muddled and your emotions are controlling you, your decisions won't reflect the rational thinking and analysis that you're normally capable of. Obviously, in some situations, you need to act instantly; when a car is speeding toward you, that's not the time to defer decision making. But when the situation permits, it's far preferable to wait till the chaos subsides – or at least to seek the advice of others before taking action.

> Do NOT make any important, irreversible decisions when you're in chaos.

Similarly, don't say or do anything you'll regret later on. It's easy to reflexively spout something while in the throes of chaos that can affect everything up to and including the rest of your life. As an IT manager, I saw this happen with Rich, a project manager in my department, who had great management potential. Rich excelled at inspiring his team members to go beyond what they believed themselves capable of. His peers liked him; his customers liked him. He was on his way to a promotion.

Until, that is, Dave ambled by. Dave was my boss's boss. He was a hefty, mean-looking dude with an occasionally brusque manner that concealed his inner teddy bear. Dave rarely ventured into the cubicles, but on this particular day, he headed straight for Rich to ask him something. When he saw the piles of clutter on Rich's desk, he made a nasty but very Dave-like wisecrack.

Normally, Rich was masterful at using his wit to defuse tension. But he was human; he didn't like being treated this way by a superior who should have been a role model. Dave's comment was a foreign element that instantly threw Rich into chaos. He responded in kind, a bad idea when facing the person who controls the direction of your career path. In that split second, Rich's future changed. When I learned what had happened, I tried to intervene on Rich's behalf, but it was too late. Rich's management prospects in this company were doomed.

What happened to Rich can happen to anyone. In chaos, people can lose the ability to think about the consequences of their actions. And so they quit their jobs, or storm out of a meeting, or reply to an angry e-mail message with an even angrier response (and hit 'send all'). Or they spout a vicious comment that, once said, they can't take back.

With practice and presence of mind, you can learn to recognize you're in chaos when you're in it. A starting point is to think about times you've been in chaos and reflect on how you reacted. If you make a mental note of the signs of chaos now, you'll stand a better chance of recognizing them when they strike.

For myself, I've learned that no matter how bad the chaos feels initially, I'm going to feel better tomorrow and I need to put off doing anything in which making a mistake or unintentionally doing something foolish could have serious repercussions.

Significant change entails a drop in productivity

Chaos usually triggers a temporary drop in productivity. This drop is hardly ideal: there's work to do and you don't have the freedom to allow things to slide as people adapt to new circumstances. Nevertheless, expecting that they will adjust without any impact on productivity is a prescription for frustration, stress and disappointment. As management consultant, Steve Smith, advises, 'Managers of groups experiencing chaos should plan for group performance to plummet during this stage.'[13]

Occasionally, I meet someone who has managed to function superbly even while in chaos. One, a financial planner known for her spreadsheet savvy, continued to achieve perfect accuracy in her work despite facing a high level of chaos. Another, a software engineer, produced some rock-solid code while another part of his life was in a shambles. The third, a risk analyst, produced twice her usual output while awaiting some potentially bad news.

Normally, though, people immersed in chaos don't perform with their customary speed, accuracy, or efficiency. If they try, as many people do because of pride, internal fortitude, or external demands, they may make more mistakes and more *serious* mistakes, resulting in botched results, project setbacks, damaged relationships, accidents, and other negative consequences.

Furthermore, dips in productivity commonly occur because it takes time for a change to unaccustomed patterns to take hold and for new habits to form. Therefore, demanding

---

[13] Steven Smith, 'The Satir Change Model,' available at *www.stevenmsmith.com/my-articles/article/the-satir-change-model.html*.

greater productivity from people who are reeling from the chaos of a major change may simply result in more and bigger problems.

Conversely, acknowledging what they're experiencing, offering support, providing guidance, and listening to their concerns can help them emerge from chaos and reach a new status quo faster.

Learning entails chaos, and chaos triggers learning

Learning is a common source of chaos. Some people thrive on this type of chaos. The temporary incompetence they experience is something they actually enjoy, or at least they are willing to tolerate it. Being – and being seen as – temporarily clumsy, slow, or error-prone as they gain competence is a minor matter to them, if not entirely irrelevant; it's simply the price to pay to develop new skills. They may even enjoy an adrenaline rush when they finally 'get it.'

Other people can't tolerate the chaos associated with this temporary incompetence, and they discontinue the activity. Daniela, a project analyst, described a fellow skeet-shooter who had this reaction. Now, skeet-shooting isn't something I'm familiar with, but apparently it's a sport many people not only enjoy, but also take lessons in so they can improve at it.[14] Daniela said her skeet-mate couldn't tolerate the mistakes she made as she attempted to advance and she chose not to increase her skeet-worthiness. Daniela, by contrast, gladly put up with the awkwardness associated with improving.

In the workplace, too, some people enjoy the learning process. Others are less enthusiastic, but go along because their job requires it of them. In time, both groups make the transition to the new way and it becomes their new normal. But inevitably, some people can't tolerate having to abandon their area of expertise and face the awkwardness of learning something new; often they seek a new position in the same company or try to find a new job elsewhere.

Actually, while learning is a source of chaos, the reverse is also true: chaos can be a source of great learning. That's because the old rules, structures, and constraints are gone. When people are in old status quo, it's easy to just coast. People are less likely to challenge the way things are; often, they can't summon the energy to tackle the matter even when they see the need.

Once the old status quo is gone, and you'll be adjusting to a new normal anyway, the future is wide open. People adopt much more of an 'oh well, why not?' attitude. It's easier to take risks and consider new possibilities that you might otherwise be unwilling to take when things are stable.

---

[14] As I now know from looking it up, skeet-shooting is a sport that simulates bird hunting and involves shooting at clay disks tossed into the air at high speeds. I'm sure that if I tried it, I'd experience *permanent* incompetence!

Practice and integration is a time of ups and downs

As a downhill skier, I know about ups and downs. You go up in the chairlift, then you ski down, then you go up, then down. It's pretty straightforward if you ignore the ups and downs associated with falling – which are actually downs and then ups.

The ups and downs of adjusting to a new status quo – 'practice and integration' in the Satir model – are not quite as methodical. In most cases, people eventually emerge from chaos. But reaching a new status quo is rarely a smooth transition from chaos. Sometimes those ups and downs are few in number and gentle; sometimes they're like a roller-coaster ride with lots of loop-de-loops.

Furthermore, this ups-and-downs experience sometimes has its own foreign elements as people adjust to new ways of doing things. For some people, each misjudgment or mistake in attempting to do something new can be as much of a foreign element as the one that created the chaos in the first place. These added foreign elements sometimes propel the individual or group back into chaos.

Eventually, a combination of practice, repetition, reinforcement, guidance, encouragement, and self-care lead to a new status quo. Often, though, reaching the new status quo is simply a matter of time. A change that may have seemed impossible to cope with initially – the new job, new manager, new location, new procedure – will, with the passage of time, become familiar. So familiar, even, that it's hard to remember when things were any other way.

Food for thought

1 Do you think it's valid to describe these nine truths as *truths*? Have you seen instances in which any of them proved not to be truths?

2 Which of these truths were already obvious to you? Which were a surprise?

3 In terms of a recent change you've observed or experienced, what helped or hindered people's ability to cope with the loss of the old way? What might have been done better?

4 Can you think of a situation in which you made an irreversible decision while in chaos and came to regret it later on? If so, how can you ensure that you will avoid repeating this situation in the future?

CHAPTER 5: DIFFERENCES IN RECEPTIVENESS TO CHANGE

Imagine a major company-wide reorganization. Reporting structures change, departments are split up or rearranged in odd ways, responsibilities are shifted around. Some people lose their jobs, some are moved laterally, some are promoted. It's as if the executives had put on blindfolds and then rearranged all the boxes in the organization chart.

That probably sounds familiar, but keep imagining. The next day, people arrive at work, go to their new work locations, and do their jobs perfectly. Best of all, everyone supports the change. Not a whimper. Not a complaint. No confusion, hesitation, or agitation. Work proceeds exactly as it should.

Okay, this is wishful thinking at its fictional best. I don't mean the reorganization, which is not so different from some that I've seen, but the reaction to it.

Back in the real world, reorganizations are more like the one my company went through when I was an IT manager. Almost every IT department changed its reporting structure, its responsibilities, its location, the customers it supported, and even its name. For weeks thereafter, wc wandered around, saying to each other, 'I know either I work for you or you work for me, but I'm not sure which.' Customers were none too pleased when IT managers called to introduce themselves and explain, 'You don't know me, but I'm now in charge of your systems.'

Happily, my department faced only a new boss, a change of name, and the addition of one customer department to support. I had terrific people in my department and, thankfully, we were able to stay together. And we didn't have to change our location. Neither did my new boss, who was now a hike-and-a-half away. But that was a minor matter in the scheme of things.

As we and our customers adjusted to new relationships, responsibilities, and channels of communication, I noticed that many people were behaving not at all like their usual selves. Some were more talkative than usual. Many were quieter. Some walked around as if in a fog. Others who were often out and about confined themselves to their cubicles and offices, as if they'd find the answer to this new organizational tangle there.

Differences such as these, it turns out, are not at all unusual during times of change. This chapter sheds light on such differences, focusing on:

1 accepting the reality of differences
2 anticipating and being tolerant of differences
3 personality differences in response to change
4 a continuum of receptivity to change
5 receptiveness to a specific change.

Accepting the reality of differences

People differ in so many ways, so it's hardly surprising that differences surface in response to change. Yet I often meet decision makers who assume that everyone experiences change identically. For example, I visited a company that had just completed a major overhaul. When I met with Gary, a finance director, he told me about the reactions he'd observed. Some people were angry. Some were cranky, acting like children. Some were enthused. Some were mumbling and grumbling. Some were complaining, but not about anything important, just about trivial matters. And some were taking the changes in their stride.

Gary seemed puzzled by these reactions and he asked me, 'Do people respond differently to change?'

Despite his lofty level, Gary seemed unaware that people vary in their receptiveness to change and will exhibit a multitude of behaviors in responding to change. And he seemed surprised by the fact that people's behavior may be more extreme than their everyday behavior, or at least different.

Gary is not alone in his narrow view of how people respond to change; I've met others high in their organizations who seem similarly unaware. But I don't believe that Gary and these others are blind to individual differences; surely, they could not have risen so high in the organization without at least a smidgen of insight into such differences. It's just (I believe) that they haven't considered how those differences will play out during the stress of change. As a result, they are surprised when employees react in numerous different ways, many of them negative.

But it's not just the upper echelons who are surprised; many people in positions from supervisor and team leader upward seem to believe that everyone affected will, and *should*, accept change. For example, Anthony, a network support engineer, insisted that everyone should accept technological change, including customers and colleagues who were not technically oriented, and that people who react otherwise simply want to remain in their comfort zone. He allowed for one exception, though: he felt that people might understandably resent an organizational change. Apparently, the types of change he believed everyone should be receptive to were those in which he himself was already skilled.

Anthony is correct about one thing: people often do want to remain in their comfort zone, particularly in the face of large-scale or high-impact change. This is a reality; it's how humans function. To think otherwise is both shortsighted and counterproductive.

> People often want to remain in their comfort zone. This is a reality; it's how humans function.

Of course, it's not just IT's customers who don't like being evicted from their comfort zone. This reaction is just as strong among IT professionals – if not, at times, stronger. Elisabeth Hendrickson, a management consultant who works with teams who are adopting agile development methods, notes that from the trenches, things are pretty confusing and seemingly random. But, she points out,

> The changes aren't actually random at all. The organization has to shift from a hierarchical command-and-control structure to a collaborative set of self-organized teams. Such a shift is inherently disruptive. And, indeed, I see all the ranges of reactions that you describe.

Whenever I publish an article on people's responses to change, I hear from readers who say things like, 'We've just gone through a huge change and the changes in behavior you've described are exactly what we're experiencing.' One person commented recently, 'We're going through a big change right now, and we're seeing the changes you listed, and more.'

It appears that despite being agents of change in the organization, IT professionals are no less jostled by change than anyone else. Almost everyone, it seems, longs for that comfort zone.

Anticipating and being tolerant of differences

If you want to manage change successfully, anticipate that you're likely to see numerous different reactions. Some of the reactions you might see include these:

1. Becky Winant, a software architect, has seen people respond with frustration, anger, indifference, fear, and finger-pointing. She has also seen people appear dazed when faced with a totally new experience when they don't have the background to know what to do next.
2. Debbie Exner, a business and personal coach, has seen people respond by persisting in doing things the old way.
3. Marco Riccioni, a freelance consultant, has seen people respond with creative and productive participation, as well as with skepticism and sabotage in the form of delaying tactics and hunting for minor errors and inaccuracies.
4. Szifra Birke, a business and rapport coach, has seen people get depressed, immobilized, angry, confused, and anxious over the emptiness they feel. Reactions also include loss of confidence and hopelessness.

5 Pamela Livingston, an education technology analyst, has seen people huddle together fearfully, speculating on what will happen next.

6 Eileen Strider, a consultant to executives, has worked with key decision makers who fail to notice their own internal thoughts and feelings, which may be trying to give them important information about the state of a change effort.

All of the above have also seen people who take change in their stride, striving to do the best they can. And, of course, many people keep their reactions inside, so there is no visible evidence of what they're experiencing.

I always encourage tolerance of the many ways people react to foreign elements, but the truth is that doing so can be difficult, as I discovered for myself on 11 September 2001. I was presenting a workshop in the US at the time, and with planes grounded, none of us could go home.

After people took the time they needed to call home and be with their emotions, we regrouped and talked about what we were feeling and how we were doing. Almost everyone was in a state of shock and distress. One fellow, however, was blasé. He said he didn't know anyone in New York and what had transpired didn't touch him. Those were his exact words: 'It doesn't touch me.'

'Seething' is the best word I can find to describe my internal reaction to this comment. How could this fellow have been so heartless, so unconcerned, so cold! But I knew that foreign elements affect people differently and here was a striking example. I thanked him for having the courage to speak his mind, and I meant it. I doubt that I'd have had the courage to express a sentiment so at odds with that of everyone around me. But I took an intense dislike to this fellow. I kept reminding myself that people respond differently to change, but, in this instance, my head couldn't overcome what my gut felt.

Personality differences in response to change

The reasons people respond differently are many, including differences in upbringing, life experiences, deep-seated fears, and personality.

Generally, information about people's upbringing, life experiences, and deep-seated fears are off limits. But widely used instruments such as the Myers-Briggs Type Indicator (MBTI)[15] offer insight into people's personality and can suggest how people who differ in terms of certain aspects of their personality might respond to change.

The MBTI focuses on four differences – which are called *preferences* in MBTI terminology – that describe how people take in information from the outside world and how they use that information to make decisions and form conclusions. These differences, briefly, including how they might influence one's reaction to change, are as follows:

1 **Extraversion/introversion**. People with a preference for *extraversion* (E) tend to think out loud and to be expressive and action-oriented. They're likely to talk about a given change and to seek ideas from many others. People with a preference for *introversion* (I) tend to be reserved, reflective, and oriented to the inner world

---

[15] The Myers-Briggs Type Indicator™ and MBTI™ are registered trademarks of Consulting Psychologists Press, Palo Alto, California. The bibliography includes some books on the MBTI and personality type.

of thoughts and ideas. Introverts are likely to work out concerns about a change privately, seeking ideas mainly from close colleagues, and communicating little until they've made a decision.

2 **Intuition/sensing**. People with a preference for *intuition* (N) tend to focus on the future, and to be drawn to theories, models, possibilities, meanings, and connections. They are likely to be interested in the big picture of a given change and to be open to trying new things. People with a preference for *sensing* (S) are detail-oriented and tend to focus on the present and the past, trusting facts, results, simplicity, and actual experience. They are likely to be happier with change that is based on what already exists and already works.

3 **Thinking/feeling**. People with a preference for *thinking* (T) tend to evaluate facts objectively, looking at both sides of an issue and the underlying principles. They are likely to approach a change analytically, concerned about the pros and cons, costs and benefits, advantages and pitfalls. People with a preference for *feeling* (F) tend to approach issues with compassion and empathy, with an emphasis on personal values and a desire for harmony and consensus. They are likely to be concerned with how the change will affect them and the people they care about.

4 **Judging/perceiving**. People with a preference for *judging* (J) tend to favor closure and control, needing to know what's happening and to have decisions made and issues settled. For a given change, they are likely to want a plan, a clear sense of priorities, and an orderly process. People with a preference for *perceiving* (P) tend to be spontaneous and comfortable with new possibilities and experiences. They are likely to want to keep options

open as long as possible and to let things evolve without too much planning.

I've deliberately used words like *tend*, *likely* and *might* in these descriptions, since it is *not* the case that everyone of a given personality type behaves a certain way in a given situation.

As a population, people with a preference for sensing are believed to be the most resistant to change and people with a preference for intuition the most receptive. In *The 7 Levels of Change*,[16] Rolf Smith cites ISFJ personalities (introverted–sensing–feeling–judging) as the most resistant to change and ENTP personalities (extraverted–intuitive–thinking–perceiving) as most accepting. He notes that since about two-thirds of people are sensing, it's reasonable to conclude that about two-thirds are resistant to change.

These personality differences come into play not only in how people respond to change, but in *how* they communicate, *when* they communicate, and *what* they communicate about, both in calm times and in times of change.

As I commented in my book *Communication Gaps and How to Close Them*, 'An awareness of these difference can help you choose how to interact with others – and how you express what you need from them – so that you can work with them amicably and productively.'[17]

Keep in mind that the MBTI describes generalities: people with a certain four-letter designation *tend* to behave a

---

[16] Rolf Smith, *The 7 Levels of Change*, The Summit Publishing Group, 1997, pp. 134–7.
[17] Naomi Karten, *Communication Gaps and How to Close Them*, Dorset House Publishing, 2002, p. 138.

certain way. But it can be presumptuous, and even harmful, to presume to know how a specific individual will respond to a specific change in a specific context. Used improperly, personality instruments can do damage.

A continuum of receptiveness to change

Consider a continuum of receptiveness to change that goes from extremely unreceptive to extremely receptive, as shown in *Figure 5*. Where would you place yourself on this continuum?

Extremely unreceptive	Extremely receptive

Figure 5: Continuum of receptivity to change

If the members of your team or department were each to put a tick mark at the point on this continuum that represents their general reaction to change, you might see a majority of tick marks on the right-hand side. If that proved to be the case, you'd have to be careful about your interpretation because people like to believe that they're open to change. They see receptiveness to change as a positive trait, and indeed it *is* a positive trait, and a career-enhancing one. Conversely, of course, being viewed as unreceptive to change is unlikely to advance anyone's career. So, on scales such as the above, people tend to rate themselves as receptive to change whether or not they actually are.

The left-hand end of the continuum

Consider the two ends of this continuum: the extremely unreceptive and the extremely receptive.

At the extreme left are people who cling to the safety and security of the status quo. Try to pull them away from what's familiar, and they hold on for dear life. Anything that jostles the orderliness of their world throws them into chaos. These people need a routine, a structure, a schedule, an agenda, an organized way of doing things. They are risk-averse; any iota of change is disruptive, if not downright mortifying. They like things to stay the way they are. If it ain't broke, don't fix it.

Now, don't misunderstand. These people can be the nicest people in the world. I know this because my father resided close to the extreme left-hand end, and everyone thought he was the nicest guy in the world. And they were right. But ordering something different on the restaurant menu from his usual choice – forget it! Falling behind his self-imposed schedule for balancing his checkbook threw him off kilter. And ... well, you get the idea.

Given structure and routine, such people are typically highly dependable. They can be counted on to dot the i's and cross the t's that others overlook. They keep things on track and ensure that nothing gets lost in the proverbial shuffle. They remember dates, keep appointments, and are never late; in fact, they'd arrive yesterday, if they could, to be sure they're on time for today's appointment. They are organized and methodical. But change is highly unsettling for them; indeed, a change that you or I barely even notice might toss them into chaos.

As I write this, I am recalling Roger, a fellow who was in one of my departments when I became its manager. Roger lived at the left-hand end of the continuum. I kid you not when I say that he arranged his paper clips in nice, even piles in his desk draw.

Structured? Roger gave new meaning to the term. He worked best with simple programming tasks. But if you wanted to know the history of any system in the company, he was the go-to guy. He'd been with the company for decades. Back then, the company was small and everyone knew everyone else. As a result, he was now on a first-name, can-I-join-you-for-lunch basis with people who were his peers back then and had since moved into the highest reaches of the company. But change discombobulated him, and I tried to keep things as even-keeled for him as I could. Maybe you've encountered people like Roger.

The right-hand end of the continuum

At the extreme right of the continuum are people who thrive on change and get bored by more than a few minutes of sameness. Routine drives them bonkers. They tend not to do things the same way twice – and certainly not the same way twice in a row. These people are always open to new possibilities. Circumstances that strike others as foreign elements may be just another ho-hum thing to them. If it ain't broke, break it so you can put it back together a different way.

In fact, these people sometimes create problems just so they'll have something to fix. They can function well in companies that are in a constant state of change, but they aren't always well received in companies with a slow and steady culture.

A fellow in one of my workshops, Josh, fitted this description. Josh worked in a start-up company, the perfect place for someone like him. He liked doing, not sitting and listening. He was highly imaginative, and needed constantly to be putting that imaginativeness into action. His antics were distracting, but also amusing. At one point, as I was presenting some serious material, he set his camera on a timed release. Then he ran over to me, said 'Smile!', and his camera took a shot of the two of us. It came out pretty good too!

Josh's behavior at times suggested conditions like attention deficit disorder, though people with this condition aren't necessarily open to change. And some would say his behavior was merely immature, though immaturity is not necessarily a characteristic of people at the right-hand end of the continuum. In any event, Josh's creativity and his ability and eagerness to explore issues from multiple angles helped his classmates succeed with projects that might otherwise have stumped them.

Receptiveness to a specific change

Of course, there's more to the picture than simply one's general receptiveness to change, because one's reactions to change are also situational. How a person reacts to a change depends on numerous factors, such as its timing and impact, the person's past experience, and the learning required to adjust to it.

> How a person reacts to a change depends on numerous factors, such as its timing and impact, the person's past experience, and the learning required to adjust to it.

An excellent example of how someone can be generally open to change but unreceptive to a specific change was Phoebe, whom I often thought of as a billing detective. If you had asked Phoebe how long she'd been with the company, she'd have said 'forever,' and (like Roger, the paper clip guy) she wasn't far off.

As a long-time member of the billing department, Phoebe had adjusted to several overhauls of the company's billing processes, as well as a vast number of other changes in the company. In recent years, she had played a key role in acceptance testing revisions to the billing system because she could be trusted to know what should happen and to notice when it didn't. Nothing got past her. She thrived on finding problems and fixing them.

But this once highly flexible system had become an ugly patchwork quilt of modifications, and every successive change to accommodate new business requirements was increasingly risky. When IT began to discuss replacing the system, Phoebe said, 'No way.' Not 'no way should a new billing system be developed,' but 'no way would she be part of it.' Phoebe's manager lobbied for a new system. But for Phoebe, enough was enough. A new system would be a massive change and she couldn't face it. She retired before she had to.

What these variations in receptiveness to change suggest is that treating everyone the same can backfire. So, in addition to reflecting on people's behavior in general, observe their reactions to any given change – their attitudes, their comments, their reactions – and you may notice differences that will offer clues about who's doing fine and who needs additional support.

Whether people are at the far ends of the continuum or, like most people, somewhere in between, significant change takes a toll. And remember: a *significant* change is one that a particular individual or group experiences as significant, whether or not you or I or anyone else agrees.

You will be more effective in helping people adjust to change if you anticipate behavioral variations in their response to it. Gary was mystified by the multitude of ways people reacted, but there's no need for you to be.

Food for thought

1 How do you view your awareness of differences in receptiveness to change? What about your superiors?
2 Where do you think the members of your work group would place themselves on the continuum of receptiveness to change?
3 Have you ever known people who you would describe as being at the extremely unreceptive or the extremely receptive ends of this continuum? If so, how did their attitude about change affect their work?
4 In what kinds of ways have people responded to changes that occurred in, or affected, your department?

CHAPTER 6: ASSESSING *YOUR* RESPONSE TO CHANGE

As they say on the airplane, put the oxygen mask on yourself before putting it on the child sitting next to you. Or as one airline put it, 'before putting it on the child sitting next to you, or the person sitting next to you who is acting like a child.' (This is an airline that understands that humor in conveying critical information increases the odds that people will actually pay attention. The wisest, most relevant communication is worthless if the people it's intended for ignore it.)

But this advice is not just oxygen-specific, nor is it limited to emergencies. The idea of taking care of yourself first is important in all aspects of life. This is the notion of self-care: that in order to be of service to others, you need to take care of yourself first, or you'll lack the wherewithal to help anyone else.

This chapter describes the importance of self-care in managing change and offers a series of questions to help you assess your own ability to cope with change. By reflecting on your own experience with change, you can become better prepared to help others cope.

The importance of self-care in managing change

When I first heard the term 'self-care,' I thought it meant I should get enough sleep and ease up on junk food. But it means much more, and this 'much more' is important in helping others cope with change.

Self-care refers to being in touch with how you're feeling: your fears, worries, hopes, and wishes; your preoccupations and pressing concerns; and the things you are telling yourself that improve, or impede, your ability to function well.

Self-care is especially important if you want to manage change successfully, because if you're bogged down by your own worries, you'll have a difficult time being fully present to others. And managers are just as susceptible to the chaos of change as the people they're managing. But managers have the special responsibility of serving as role models. They demonstrate by example how to deal with difficult, stressful, or unusual circumstances. Remaining mindful of this responsibility while in chaos can be difficult for any manager.

In *Powerful Project Leadership*, management consultant and author, Wayne Strider, presents the concept of starting before you start, a form of self-care that he describes as the zeroth step. This notion of a zeroth step may appear to be a paradox. But, as Strider points out, it's not a paradox because, no matter where you start – whether working on a project, managing change, or anything else – something came before.

Strider explains that you can start 'shaping processes and outcomes before the project starts, or reshaping them as the project progresses.'[18] The same is true for managing change: you can start shaping processes and outcomes even before the change begins, and reshape them as the change effort progresses. Strider describes the zeroth step as 'a

---

[18] Wayne Strider, *Powerful Project Leadership*, Management Concepts, 2002, pp. 21–2.

journey inward – a journey inside you, a reflection, a private interview with yourself.' It's difficult to think of any important undertaking that can't benefit from attention to the zeroth step.

Therefore, if you seek to guide others through change, a useful zeroth step would be to examine your own response to change. Using the terminology from the Satir change model, I offer the following questions as a basis for your self-assessment. (For a refresher on this terminology, *see Chapter 3*.)

The questions are in four sections:

1 changes you've faced in the past
2 your general reaction to change
3 changes you're facing right now
4 managing change in others.

Note that there are no wrong answers. And there's no rating system.

As you review these questions, keep in mind that chaos is a normal response to change. Ignore anyone who attempts to persuade you otherwise, or who insists, 'You should be over it by now.' False! There may be things you can do to help yourself emerge from chaos sooner, but you're over it when *you* are over it.

Changes you've faced in the past

Think of three or four changes you've experienced that were memorable. If possible, consider changes of different kinds, such as positive and negative changes, expected and unexpected changes, or big and small changes. You might find it useful to make a list of some of the more memorable ones; it may be that patterns will emerge in how you cope.

1 Of the changes you've identified, which ones (if any) did you sail through with minimal or no chaos at all?

2 Of the changes you've identified, which ones were foreign elements that propelled you into chaos?

3 Can you detect any differences in the types of changes that you handled effortlessly compared with those that caused chaos? What distinguished them from each other?

4 In the changes you've experienced, what kinds of things have been foreign elements for you?

5 When faced with these foreign elements, how did you respond? What were your initial reactions?

6 What was chaos like for you? How did it affect your mental and emotional stability, your interactions with others, your ability to carry out your responsibilities, and how you felt about yourself?

7 What might people have noticed about you when you've been in chaos? In what ways, if any, might you have behaved or functioned differently from what's typical for you?

8 When you were in chaos, how did others help or hinder your adjustment to a new status quo?

9 Do you recall any transforming ideas that have helped you emerge from chaos?

10 What do you remember about the experience of practice and integration as you adjusted to the change?
11 When you reached a new status quo, how did the experience that you came through appear to you?
12 How did your experience with these changes map onto the Satir change model?
13 Does your view of any of these change experiences look different now than when they originally occurred?

Your general response to change

Given your responses to the preceding questions, these next questions may help you gain some insight into how you respond to change in general:

1 In general, what kinds of circumstances and situations do you experience as foreign elements? What kinds of things shake you up or throw you off kilter? Do these things have anything in common?
2 When faced with foreign elements, how do you typically respond? What is your initial reaction?
3 What might you do so that these situations have less power over you as foreign elements?
4 What is chaos like for you? How does it affect your ability to think clearly, to carry out your responsibilities, to be productive, and to get along with others?
5 When you're in chaos, what kinds of things do you tell yourself that are helpful or harmful to your well-being? What kinds of self-talk do you engage in?
6 When you're in chaos, what kinds of support do you need? In general, what do you find most helpful or unhelpful in coping with the chaos?

7 What might people notice about you when you are in chaos? In what ways, if any, might you behave or function differently from what's typical for you?
8 What can you do to take care of yourself – to be good to yourself – when in chaos?
9 What might you do to minimize the duration and intensity of the chaos that you experience?
10 When you've been in chaos, what kinds of transforming ideas have helped you emerge from chaos?
11 What sources of transforming ideas might help you that you have previously overlooked or dismissed?
12 What do you recall about the experience of practice and integration as you've adjusted to the change?
13 What do you notice about your attitude and well-being once you've achieved a new status quo?
14 Overall, what can you do differently to improve the way you handle change?

Changes you're facing right now

Now, draw from what you've learned from the previous questions, and from whatever you now know (or already knew) about change, in order to ease any turbulence you're experiencing with current changes. Consider these questions:

1 What is your state of chaos right now? What foreign elements caused the chaos? What kinds of things are increasing or decreasing that chaos?
2 How is the chaos you are experiencing affecting you mentally and emotionally?

3 What might others notice about your behavior, attitudes, and ability to do your job?
4 In terms of this chaos, what do you have control over and what do you not?
5 What are you telling yourself about this state of chaos? Are there any *shoulds* or *musts* that need readjustment?
6 What can you do for yourself – without needing assistance from anyone else – to reduce the intensity and the duration of the chaos you're experiencing?
7 What kinds of support will help you emerge from chaos? What do you need to do to gain that support?
8 What kinds of transforming ideas might help you that you've rejected or not considered? What might you do to enable new transforming ideas to surface?
9 What can you do to be tolerant (or at least to avoid being intolerant or impatient) with yourself during the ups and downs of practice and integration?
10 When you've achieved a new status quo, what will you do to learn from the experience?

Managing change in others

This section has only one question:

1 Given what you've learned or realized in reviewing these questions, what can you do – and what *will* you do – to guide others through change in a way that will minimize their chaos and expedite their journey to a new status quo?

The remaining chapters offer numerous suggestions in response to this final question.

You might find it helpful to draw from these questions, along with any others of your own choosing, and use them as the basis for a discussion with teams or groups that are facing change – or might at some future time.

Food for thought

1 What surprised you, if anything, about your responses to these self-assessment questions?

2 What do you realize now about your responses to change that you weren't fully aware of previously?

3 What other questions would be appropriate in assessing how you cope with change? And how would you answer them?

CHAPTER 7: BUILDING A FOUNDATION FOR MANAGING CHANGE

During times of change, there's invariably a great deal you can't control. But you'll be in a much better position to manage change, if you do certain things during calmer times that you *can* control and that are much more difficult to accomplish during the turbulence of chaos.

Three things you *can* control are:

1 creating trusting relationships

2 establishing team norms

3 conducting temperature readings.

This chapter offers some thoughts about why you'd benefit from undertaking these efforts, and how to do so.

Creating trusting relationships

Building trust is the number one prerequisite to leading a successful change effort, and it's a prerequisite that's often overlooked in the rush to implement change. Why does trust matter? Because it determines whether or not people believe what you tell them. When change comes along, people immediately start to wonder:

1 How will it affect me?

2 What will happen to my job?

3 Will I be able to handle it?

4 What if I *can't* handle it?

5 What are they keeping from me?

6 Who is going to help me?

When people trust you, they are inclined to consider your ideas and follow your lead. They are receptive to your ideas and advice. They give you the benefit of the doubt. They attribute positive intentions to your actions, even if those actions are not what they would wish for. Trust creates a foundation for a relationship that can withstand the stresses of change.

Conversely, if people don't trust you, they are likely to discount, dismiss, or ignore anything you say and do. They'll see malevolent intentions in your actions. They'll perceive a hidden agenda in your actions – and a negative hidden agenda at that. And they'll withhold information you need to do your job. This is particularly the case if you're a manager and your employees don't trust you.

Festering distrust feeds on itself. If someone distrusts you and you do nothing to reverse that distrust, it will only get worse. And without trust, accomplishing almost anything is difficult. Managing change is especially difficult because people are already in a shaky condition, unsure of what's happening and how it will affect them.

Fair warning: if you have an untrustworthy reputation, people will interpret anything you say and do with suspicion. This was the case in a company in which morale among IT employees was plunging, due in large part to their distrust in their management. Fortunately, when a new

CIO, Chet, took over, he recognized that no improvement in employee satisfaction would be possible without a rebuilding of trust. Accordingly, Chet invited employees to volunteer for an employees-only team (no management allowed) whose role would be to identify what was causing the lack of trust and recommend solutions. Chet brought me in as a consultant to facilitate and support the efforts of the volunteer team.

Through discussions with each other and interviews with their coworkers, the team members pinpointed deeply flawed communication as the biggest cause of the distrust. For example, while certain managers openly discussed plans, decisions, and upcoming changes with their employees, other managers withheld this information. But even when managers were forthcoming, it seemed as if no two of them told their staff the same thing. At times, information on a particular matter arrived from multiple sources, with so many inconsistencies that employees didn't know who or what to believe.

Making matters worse, many people were afraid to speak up to their management for fear that their input would be used against them.

The speed of trust

In *The Speed of Trust*, Stephen M. R. Covey offers a simple formula to make the impact of trust more quantifiable and tangible.[19] Trust, according to Covey, affects two outcomes: speed and cost. When trust goes down, speed will go down and costs will go up.

---

[19] Stephen M. R. Covey, *The Speed of Trust*, Free Trust, 2006, p. 13.

Covey presents this relationship visually as:

↓ Trust = ↓ Speed ↑ Cost

Conversely, when trust goes up, speed will go up and costs will go down:

↑ Trust = ↑ Speed ↓Cost

It doesn't take an extreme stretch of the imagination to appreciate that the absence of trust causes change efforts to take longer and cost more.

In contrast, if you're known for playing it straight, telling the truth, being responsive, being open to the perspectives of others, and treating people with respect, they will accept that you're telling them what you can and not needlessly withholding information. And if you can't tell them all you know, they'll trust you when you tell them that you'll let them know as soon as you can.

How to lose trust quickly

Trust is fragile. It can take months, or even years, to build a trustworthy reputation, and barely minutes to damage that reputation. As I once learned at first hand, sometimes it doesn't even take minutes. On the first day of one of my workshops, people had formed teams which, I explained, would remain intact throughout the workshop. This first day included several team activities, which helped team members get to know each other and work together.

After presenting the Satir change model on Day 2, I asked the group to divide into their teams to discuss applications of the model in their companies. But I wanted to help them understand chaos at a gut level, not merely as an abstract concept, so I hatched a plan: at the end of the discussion period, I announced that they would now form new teams. Imagine how you'd feel if you'd connected with people you really liked and you didn't want to sever that connection and team up with people who were still nearly strangers.

Please understand: I wasn't actually planning to disrupt the original teams. My thought was that this announcement would be a foreign element that would create the visceral experience of a minor bit of chaos. And my intention was to tell them, maybe 30 seconds later, that of course they could remain in their original teams.

So much for intentions. Upon hearing my announcement, some participants immediately became angry. Some refused to abandon their teams. The members of one team clung together, daring me to try to separate them. A few, interestingly, became energized about forming new teams. Taken aback by the intensity of these reactions, I lost track of time. Perhaps 60 seconds passed, or maybe 90, but whatever it was, it was too long.

By the time I explained that this was simply a simulation of chaos and that teams would remain intact, some people had lost trust in me for reneging on my promise. At the same time, the people who were eager to create new teams were disappointed, even annoyed. So, whereas many participants became upset because I'd told them they'd be forming new teams, these few became upset because they weren't really going to be forming new teams. Everyone had taken me at my word.

Fortunately, almost everyone eventually came around to appreciating my intentions, despite my clumsy way of carrying them out. Still, every time I introduced an exercise or class activity, several people challenged my intentions and asked if there was a trick involved.

This was a huge lesson for me. Letting people down about something that's important to them can be a quick trip to distrust. I had underestimated what an intense foreign element my announcement about creating new teams would be. Needless to say, they learned a lot about chaos that day. So did I, feeling chaos throughout the rest of the workshop as I attempted to regain their trust.

But just think about it: if a 'minor' foreign element in a 90-second simulation in the safe setting of a classroom can trigger such a huge bout of chaos, what does it suggest about the likely level of chaos during a major change in a large company?

How to earn trust, and why it's not so easy

The common wisdom is that trust is something you have to earn; however, this is an oversimplification. Several factors influence how quickly you're able to gain trust, and while some of these factors are within your control, there are others that aren't.

One factor that's outside your control is how trusting the other party is. People develop trust at different rates in different situations. Some people enter new relationships trusting others and maintain that trust until circumstances convince them otherwise. And even then, they may remain trusting.

Other people are the opposite: they enter new relationships with a tendency to distrust until circumstances and the passage of time convince them otherwise. If you attempt to gain their trust too quickly, they may see you as scheming or insincere. The problem, of course, is that you can't necessarily discern which people are which.

Furthermore, for each of us, trust has boundaries, but where we each locate those boundaries varies with the situation. And regardless of the situation, your boundaries and mine are likely to differ. You might trust me to keep you away from the edge of a cliff, but not trust me to find the bugs in your code. I might trust you to troubleshoot my misbehaving laptop, but not to take my new car for a spin in rush-hour traffic.

Another factor you have little control over is context. If you're in a group known for being untrustworthy, you can suffer distrust by association. For example, an IT division I once worked in had a miserable reputation due to the poor performance of just a few departments. Although my own department and several others did good work and had happy customers, many customers didn't distinguish one IT department from another and roundly distrusted them all.

It didn't help that one IT department had the gall to assign a major project a name whose abbreviation was ASAP, best known as the abbreviation for *as soon as possible*. But not only did the department not deliver as soon as possible, it didn't deliver at all.

If you work in an organization that has an untrustworthy reputation, you can still earn trust through your own actions and behavior, but it's likely to take a lot longer than it would in a trusted organization. And, unfortunately, it takes much longer to rebuild a reputation for trustworthiness than it takes to lose it. When people distrust, they adopt a 'wait-and-see' mindset until they're convinced that any improved behavior in those they've distrusted is real and permanent. It is much easier to keep the trust you've earned than to lose it and gain it back.

> It's *much* easier to keep the trust you've earned than to lose it and gain it back.

What you **can** *control*

What you *can* control is yourself. Keep in mind Jerry Weinberg's First Law of Trust: 'Nobody but you cares about the reason you let another person down.'[20] Ultimately, you earn trust by what you say and how you behave – and this is true whether or not others are trusting by nature, and whether or not the context is viewed as trustworthy. It's not any one thing that earns the trust of others, but rather a pattern of behavior that says, 'I'm someone you can trust.'

[20] Gerald M. Weinberg, *The Secrets of Consulting*, Dorset House Publishing, 1985, p. 196.

This pattern of behavior entails such things as meeting your commitments (or letting others know in advance if you can't); being friendly; communicating coherently; listening attentively; being open to other people's views; accepting responsibility for your mistakes; appreciating the efforts of others; treating people with respect; and exhibiting honesty, integrity, and empathy. And if you want others to trust you, you have to be willing to trust them, and to act accordingly.

Payson Hall, a systems engineer and consulting project manager, emphasizes that without proper care, relationships decay. Hall advises managers to have frequent one-on-one communication with employees. He also recommends that managers ask for input and *listen to it* before making decisions. And managers need to avoid shooting the messenger who brings bad news. Shoot the messenger, he cautions, and problems will still occur, but people will stop telling you about them.[21]

Basically, earning trust is a matter of doing the everyday things you should be doing anyway. And, happily, you can do them without needing anyone's support, approval, or go-ahead. Of course, having earned trust, you can't get lazy; you have to keep on behaving in a way that justifies a continuation of that trust.

Demonstrating that you're trustworthy won't keep people from going into chaos when a change comes along, but it can go a long way toward minimizing the duration and intensity of that chaos. But if people view you as untrustworthy, they may experience anything you say as yet

---

[21] Payson Hall, 'Tending Communication Paths,' in *Better Software Magazine*, October 2007, pp. 16–17.

another foreign element heaped upon those associated with the change itself.

If you have reason to believe that you're seen as untrustworthy, start immediately to build trust (or rebuild it if you once had it but lost it), so that you can manage change successfully when it comes along. It will come in handy, even if you're fortunate enough to have an extended period free of change.

Establishing team norms

Team norms, like trust, are easier to establish when things are calm than in the midst of change. Team norms concern how members of a group will communicate and interact with each other. The group can be a department, a project team, a committee, or any other group of people who are working together toward a common goal. For simplicity, I'm referring to these various groups as a 'team' and the norms as 'team norms.'

Norms help people agree on how they'd like to get along with each other before misunderstandings, squabbles, and stressful situations emerge. It's not impossible for a team mired in chaos to create norms, but it's much harder. And since the norms can help a team accomplish its goals, they're useful even if chaos never arises.

Here are some of the norms that teams I've worked with have found helpful:

1 Strive to understand each other's perspectives.

2 Resolve problems without blaming others.

3 Respect 'do not disturb' signs on people's cubicles.

4 If you make a commitment you can't keep, let the parties know as soon as possible.
5 If you don't understand something, ask for clarification.
6 If you see a problem, report it.
7 Treat each other's concerns as valid, even if you don't agree with them.
8 If you detect a conflicting understanding among team members, let them know.
9 Notice what's going well, not just what's going wrong.

Norms can address everyday communication issues, such as how team members will stay in contact, how they'll communicate urgent information among themselves and to other parties, which communication channel (face to face, phone, e-mail, etc.) to use in different situations, and how to improve e-mail readability.

It may also be appropriate to have norms that specify when *not* to use e-mail. As Pamela Livingston, author of *1-to-1 Learning: Laptop Programs That Work*, notes, 'E-mail can be forwarded and copied and edited: if you don't want the message posted next to the water cooler, don't send it. Use a different vehicle.'

Attempting to create norms when a team is in chaos can exacerbate the chaos. By having these norms in place before a given change emerges, team members can gain experience in adhering to them, questioning them, and adjusting them. Any conflict that arises is then more likely to be surfaced, discussed, and resolved before frustrations fester and tensions mount.

In my experience, it's not just the norms themselves that help teams function more smoothly; it's also the setting of the norms. The process of establishing norms gives team members an opportunity to tell each other what's important to them about team functioning. For a description of how to create team norms, see my article, 'Creating Team Norms,' available at *www.stickyminds.com/s.asp?F=S6736_COL_2*.

Conducting temperature readings

A temperature reading is a tool created by Virginia Satir that helps teams reduce tensions; improve relationships; and surface information, ideas, and feelings that might otherwise be suppressed. It's a communication tool I enjoy teaching because it's so effective, especially in times of change. As with team norms, it's better to introduce temperature readings during times of relative calm, rather than when everyone is thrashing around in chaos.

Some teams conduct temperature readings weekly, some monthly. Some do it at the end of a project or at key milestones during the project. It consists of five segments:

1 **Appreciations**. During busy workdays – and especially during times of change – teams tend to overlook the positive things they've experienced. In this first segment, everyone in the team who would like to can thank or appreciate one or more others in the team. An appreciation can be for anything, whether large or small, and whether critical to the team's efforts or simply a kind word.

   In giving an appreciation, rather than speaking to the rest of the team about the person, speak directly to them, such as by saying 'I appreciate you because ...' or 'Thank you for ...' or 'I liked it when you ...' Although some people initially feel awkward giving or receiving appreciations, most people eventually discover how satisfying it can be both to give and to receive.

2 **New information**. Often, one or another team member has information that others may be unaware of, may need to know, or would simply find interesting. Anyone with such information can offer it during this segment. During times of change, this segment can help to surface and resolve the rumors that are floating around.

3 **Puzzles**. This segment provides a sanctioned opportunity for team members to describe something they find unclear or confusing and would like explained. Sometimes, other team members can quickly provide the needed clarification during the temperature reading. If it'll take more than a few minutes, they can agree to meet afterwards.

4 **Complaints with recommendations**. In the workplace, complaints are usually unwelcome. This segment, however, explicitly *invites* complaints. But, unlike a gripe session, this segment is constructive: the person voicing the complaint offers a recommendation for addressing the complaint or requests recommendations from the group.

5 **Hopes and wishes**. In this final segment, team members who would like to can express a hope or wish pertinent to the team, to its members, or to issues of interest to the team.

A manager or any team member can lead a temperature reading. Some teams like to rotate the role so that everyone can gain experience leading it. A full temperature reading takes from 15 minutes to an hour or more, depending on the size of the team and its circumstances.

If there's not enough time to do a full temperature reading, focus on whichever segments will be most helpful to the team. For example, if there's been an unusual amount of confusion, puzzles may offer some clarification. If people are feeling stressed, appreciations may help to energize the group.

The terminology of temperature readings is very flexible and you can tweak it to fit your team or company culture. If you don't like 'appreciations' or 'hopes and wishes,' you can call them 'looking back' and 'looking forward.' You can replace 'information' with 'rumor stifling,' or replace 'puzzles' with 'mysteries and enigmas.' For that matter, if 'temperature reading' itself is a name that wouldn't go over well, call it a 'team check-in,' or a 'monthly review,' or something else.

By the way, don't feel obligated to wait for a temperature reading to express an appreciation. Do it when you think of it. It's a wonderful habit and a highly contagious one. And during times of change, people can really appreciate being appreciated.

Food for thought

1 Think of someone in your company whom you trust. What led you to trust that person?
2 Conversely, think of someone you don't trust. What led you to distrust that person?
3 How might you go about establishing team norms?
4 How do you think your coworkers might respond to participating in a temperature reading?

CHAPTER 8: INTRODUCING CHANGE THOUGHTFULLY

In introducing change, managers tend to focus on what is changing – that is, the technical aspects of the change. In the process, they often overlook, or give too little attention to, the human aspects of the change. The human aspects are the focus of this chapter. In particular:

1 Identifying who will be affected by a change.
2 Minimizing the compounding effect of chaos.
3 Not withholding news of looming foreign elements.
4 Explaining the reasons for a change.

Identifying who will be affected by a change

Who will be affected by a given change? It's easy to answer this question narrowly, without considering the broader impact. For example, if a team is changing its development method, obviously the developers are affected. But who else? The answer may include numerous parties who interact with the developers, as well as anyone who depends on the work of the developers or on whom the developers themselves depend.

In the opening case study in Chapter 1, the team responsible for the enterprise-wide desktop upgrade focused on the technical aspects of the change, as well they should. But neither Glenn and his team nor Russell, the CIO, gave more than a passing thought to the customers who would be the primary recipients of the change. As a result, they didn't consider how these people would be affected.

Clearly, the question of *who* is important; you can't fully plan *how* you will implement a change without considering the people who will be affected by it. Wait, that's not quite true; Glenn's upgrade and countless other changes are proof of that. But if you want to minimize the duration and intensity of the chaos that the change triggers (and avoid the unintended consequences, such as the damage to IT's reputation, as in Glenn's situation), you need to consider the human impact of the change.

The question of who will be affected by a change needs to take into account both those directly affected and those indirectly affected. For example, a round of layoffs will obviously affect the people who will lose their jobs. But it will also affect the people remaining, especially those who have to absorb the work of their departed colleagues.

Adrian Segar, a former IT consultant, notes,

> Unless you can identify who, specifically, is part of your constituency, and who is not part of your constituency, you will have a heck of a time communicating with your constituency. Consider all those who will be affected directly or indirectly, those who think they will be affected, and those who need to be, or want to be, involved. Figure out who these parties are at the *start* of the project.[22]

Segar knows whereof he speaks. In one of the final consulting engagements of his IT career, he neglected to think about who might be affected by his work and the project suffered as a result.

Start by considering the people who are the immediate targets of the change. But, in addition, consider who the

---

[22] Presentation, 'The Systematic Development of Informed Consent,' by Adrian Segar, edAccess Conference, 25 June 2008.

immediate targets interact with in the course of their work. Then go further and consider who else in or outside the company is affected, or might be affected. Think broadly. Make a list. Even if you suspect the impact will be minor for some individuals or groups, include them on the list.

Once you consider the *who*, you can begin to consider the rest of the *what*; that is, what do you need to do to prepare these people, to inform them, to ease the experience for them? You can ask how they might experience the change and what aspects of their work must be taken into account.

Ideally, you can simply ask these people directly. Even without his CIO's backing, Glenn might have contacted several department managers to discuss the upcoming upgrade. When you talk to the parties who will be affected by a change, you invariably learn about aspects of their work that you were unaware of. Thus informed, you can make decisions that will enable you to implement the change more responsibly.

> When you talk to the parties who will be affected by a change, you will learn about aspects of their work that you were unaware of.

I'm not under any illusion that senior management will contact the victims of their next grand layoff and ask them, psychiatrist-style, 'How does this make you feel?' But I'm hopeful that in future instances of change, such as Glenn's upgrade, those in charge will pay attention to the human impact of the change, easing the toll it takes both on those on the receiving end of the change and on those who drive the change.

Minimizing the compounding effect of chaos

This issue concerns the timing of the introduction of a change or the start of a change effort. Often, the timing is dictated by business cycles, seasonal variations, external factors, governmental cycles, regulatory mandates, or other factors over which you have no say. And sometimes, the timing of the start of a change effort is driven by when it must be completed: before year-end, for example, or before a piece of legislation comes into effect.

But sometimes, you do have some say about the timing. And if the change is likely to be a foreign element, it may be better to delay its introduction if those it will affect are already in considerable chaos from a previous foreign element.

For example, the impact of introducing new processes may be much more severe when people are reeling from the impact of a merger, a company takeover, or the worldwide financial turmoil playing out as I write this. (Keeping one eye on the fluctuating stock market doesn't make writing about change any easier.) One overly ambitious company I heard about simultaneously introduced a new marketing strategy, new personnel, and new online technology – and, amazingly, only a short time before their busy Christmas selling season. In their haste to change too much at one time, their efforts backfired badly, resulting in lost sales, irritated customers, and damaged morale.

The way people respond to a given foreign element depends at least in part on where they are – old status quo, chaos, practice and integration, or new status quo – in terms of other changes.

The addition of a new foreign element when people are still reeling from the chaos from a previous foreign element can create a 'double whammy,' as software-testing consultant Fiona Charles describes it. The risk is that the cumulative effect of multiple foreign elements will significantly increase the intensity and duration of the chaos people experience, resulting in more than they can handle and prolonging the attainment of a new status quo.

By the time people are in the practice and integration stage, they are more able, both mentally and emotionally, to tolerate a new foreign element. And once they've achieved a new status quo, they are best equipped to contend with a new foreign element.

Obviously, people may be dealing with chaos that you know nothing about in their personal lives. Even at work, you can't be expected to know the level of chaos everyone is experiencing. But by being sensitive to the matter of timing – considering the feasibility of introducing a new foreign element tomorrow rather than today, next month rather than this month – you may be able to minimize the chaos people experience, and that will be to your benefit as well as to theirs.

A question that often comes up when I raise this issue of timing is the advisability of introducing several foreign elements at one time if they are of a similar kind. Might it not be best to do all of them at once, and cope with a bout of monumental chaos, rather than to wait for the chaos of each new initiative to settle down before moving on to the next?

Indeed, it's sometimes better to have one big episode of chaos and to work through it than several smaller episodes which, though less stressful, can lead to chaos fatigue.

At other times, a little at a time may be smarter. In *Agile Software Development in the Large*, author Jutta Eckstein cautions that in introducing agile processes into software development teams, 'Never introduce everything at once, because this will more than likely overwhelm all those involved.'[23] For example, if the rate of bugs is unacceptably high, she suggests that you start by unit testing, followed by refactoring.[24] If coding standards are too complex, the best starting point may be to simplify the coding standards.

Unfortunately, there's no one best way and no set of timing criteria that you can count on to guide you. You have to use your judgment and do the best you can. Just keep in mind that it's better to consider the potential pitfalls before heaving the next foreign element into the mix, than to scramble to recover from the impact of the resulting chaos.

Not withholding news of a looming foreign element

This is another timing issue, one that concerns the timing of the notification of a change. The sooner employees know about a forthcoming foreign element, the sooner they can find their way through the resulting chaos.

Of course, informing employees in advance is not always feasible, such as when the premature news of a foreign element could drive customers away or send the company's stock price into a nosedive. But withholding information about an upcoming change in the name of kindness ('It'll be bad enough as it is; I want to spare them any additional

---

[23] Jutta Eckstein, *Agile Software Development in the Large*, Dorset House Publishing, 2004, p. 29.

[24] Refactoring is the process of improving the source code to make it easier for the software team to manage and modify.

pain') usually backfires because it amounts to treating adults like children. Talk about a trust-buster!

> Withholding information about an upcoming change in the name of kindness amounts to treating adults like children.

Withholding bad news may spare you from dealing with employees' reactions, but, from the employees' perspective, such withholding is dishonest, thoughtless, and unkind. And withholding bad news because it just didn't occur to you that it would matter to others is a blatant sign of disrespect.

I saw a glaring example of this disrespect in a company that was facing layoffs. On Monday, Troy, a vice president, notified employees that on Friday he'd announce who would be terminated. Productivity plummeted as fear and anxiety gripped the entire division.

On Friday morning, Troy learned that he'd have to delay the announcement until the following Monday due to some legal matters. But he told employees nothing at all until his administrative assistant pleaded with him, in mid-afternoon, to let everyone know that the announcement had been deferred until Monday. It just plain hadn't occurred to him that telling people would be the right thing to do. (Fill in your choice of adjectives for Troy here.)

Of course, it's natural to want to withhold bad news. When schedules slip and technical problems arise, most IT professionals don't relish the prospect of having to tell their customers. Besides, why say anything, if, with a little extra effort, the project can recover and customers needn't know?

But often the project can't recover, and when customers then learn about the situation, they become angry, and understandably so.

In general, most people would prefer to hear bad news sooner rather than later if it will affect their ability to do their jobs properly. Customers I've interviewed while consulting to IT organizations have often mentioned their frustration over not being kept informed about changes in IT's ability to deliver as agreed.

I well remember the words of one such customer, who said, with some vehemence, 'IT needs to understand that we have responsibilities and accountabilities as well. We need to know what's happening, so we can make adjustments at our end.' In effect, they were saying that the sooner they know about a foreign element, the sooner they can deal with the resulting chaos and get past it.

This issue of informing people about an upcoming change has an ethical component which surfaced during my presentation on managing change at a software conference. In a lively exchange, audience members debated whether it's not only dishonest, but also unethical, for a manager to refrain from giving employees news that affects them and that he's actually free to disclose. The majority felt that the ethical thing to do, almost always, is to disclose the information, even it means contending with the resulting reactions. This is an issue you might want to think about.

Explaining the reasons for a change

Upon learning about a major change, most people quickly become preoccupied, not by the reasons for the change, but by what it means for them. But not providing the reasons for the change can be a mistake, because in the absence of an explanation, people draw their own conclusions and the rumor mill grinds into action.

Furthermore, in the absence of information, people begin to distrust those in the know – as well as those they assume to be in the know, whether or not they actually are. Just as arbitrarily delaying the news of a foreign element is a sign of disrespect, arbitrarily withholding explanations of a change is also a sign of disrespect.

A preferable alternative is to offer an explanation – and make sure it's truthful; people can see through fictionalized explanations. But don't go into tedious, mind-numbing detail. Consider the executive who thought it appropriate to enlighten employees with 90-minute, PowerPoint®-intensive, spreadsheet-laden account of why the company's primary call center was going to be outsourced.

To his credit, he meant well. He believed that if employees understood the financial justification for the decision, they'd be more receptive. But he overwhelmed them with details. As a result of the unexpected news and the wallop of the resulting chaos, they became immediately lost in thought, figuring out how the change would affect them.

The executive might have done better by offering a brief overview, summarizing the decision and the reasons for it, and how it would affect call center employees, along with a source of additional details for those who wanted them.

But, at least, by being open about what was going on, he retained the respect of his employees, even as they coped with the implications of the change.

This executive's handling of this huge decision was consistent with the forthright behavior he was known for. In an age of rampant disrespect for the people affected by a change, this is not a trivial matter.

Food for thought

1. In a recent change that you participated in, what steps were taken to identify the parties that might be affected? Were any important parties overlooked?
2. Can you think of instances in which the news of a change was either withheld too long or introduced at a time of major chaos? What was the result? What lessons do you draw about the timing of future changes?
3. What has been done well, or poorly, in recent changes in terms of explaining the reasoning for the change?

CHAPTER 9: TALKING TO THE PEOPLE AFFECTED BY CHANGE

This chapter and the next one offer specific suggestions for reducing the duration and intensity of the chaos associated with change. I've touched on many of these ideas in previous chapters, but these two chapters pull them all together in one place.

This chapter focuses on the following suggestions for communicating to and with the people who are coping with change:

1 Seek understanding.

2 Talk to the naysayers.

3 Reduce the uncertainty associated with change.

4 Communicate even in the absence of information.

5 Communicate about information you can't disclose.

6 Explain the impact of a change on those affected.

7 Invite people to contribute ideas about the change.

8 Give people a sense of control.

9 Help people understand each other's perspectives.

Seek understanding

Sadly, many people believe that everyone views the world exactly as they do. The rest of us know better, but in times of chaos, when our thinking is muddled, we sometimes fall victim to the exact same belief. Trapped by this belief, we conclude that if other people's reactions don't match our own, there must be something wrong with *them*.

Organizational consultant, Margaret Wheatley, provides guidance to help us steer clear of these misguided beliefs. In her book *Leadership and the New Science*, she explains that in any group, there are as many interpretations of everything that happens as there are people in the group. As a matter of fact, no two people see the world in exactly the same way. This is true, she points out, even when the members of the group have a shared identity.

In promoting a given change, therefore, she aims to stay open to the different reactions that people exhibit rather than immediately categorizing them as resisters or allies (Wheatley admits this is not always easy). When we do the same, we set the stage to expect diverse responses. In the process, we avoid assigning conversation-stopping labels to these reactions, and we are able to seek an understanding of how people are experiencing what's happening.

As Wheatley points out, once we apply labels to people, we lose any curiosity we might otherwise have had about why they are behaving as they do. As a result, we fail to discover common issues and concerns that might be important to everyone involved in the change. She points out, 'We are quick to assign people to a typology and then dismiss them, as if we really knew who they were.'[25] Furthermore, the urgent need to implement important changes leads people to seek scapegoats. We quickly blame those we label as resisters for our inability to move the change forward.

Conversation is central to Wheatley's view of what needs to happen to enable change to take place. When we engage in

[25] Margaret Wheatley, *Leadership and the New Science*, Berrett-Koehler Publishers, p. 150.

conversation – when we actually talk to each other about what we're experiencing and why we're responding as we are – we can avoid applying divisive categories to each other and find ways to work together.

Talk to the naysayers

Conversation is fine, but if your goal is to inspire change, it's not enough to talk only to those who already agree with you. In describing the challenges he experienced during a consulting project for a school, Adrian Segar, a former IT consultant, noted that while the technical staff on one campus supported the project, the technical staff on the other were dead set against it.

In retrospect, Segar realized that he focused most of his attention on the people who supported him. Who can blame him? They were happy with his work, so it was easy for him to hang out with them. He admits that he even joined them in complaining about how unreasonable the people at the other campus were.

But why didn't he at least approach the people on this other campus? The reason was simple: it would have been scary.

Segar acknowledges, 'I was scared to hear what they might have to say. So I played it safe. For years.'[26]

> If your goal is to inspire change, it's not enough to talk only to those who already agree with you.

After studying with Hans and Annemarie Bleiker (*www.ipmp.com*), an engineer and an anthropologist who have studied why many projects never get implemented and what can be done to improve the odds of success, Segar saw the situation in a different light. In any major undertaking, we tend to divide the people affected into three categories: those who support the effort, those who are neutral, and those who silently oppose it. As many of us might have done, it was to these categories of people that Segar devoted his energy and effort. But the real problem is one additional category: the NIMBYs – Not in My Back Yard – who have an 'over-my-dead-body' view of the change. And this is where attention needs to be focused.

Approaching fervent naysayers takes courage. Their very existence can drive you into chaos. Unfortunately, few change efforts can succeed without their support. The very fact of initiating a conversation may help show that you're interested in their perspective and willing to listen to their concerns. And sometimes, your persistence in getting to know them and helping them know you will soften their opposition and enable your effort to move forward.

[26] Presentation, 'The Systematic Development of Informed Consent,' by Adrian Segar, edAccess Conference, 25 June 2008.

Reduce the uncertainty associated with change

The uncertainty people experience during chaos is one of its most oppressive qualities. This is true even in relatively trivial situations, as I learned one winter on the way to a long-planned ski trip. With a baggage cart piled high with luggage, we headed for our rental car. Somewhere along the way, my ski boots disappeared. (Notice that I didn't say I dropped my boots or I let them fall off the baggage cart. When foreign elements strike – and this was certainly one – we often slip into ineffective communication stances such as blaming. I blamed my boots for disappearing.)

We searched everywhere. No boots. I was in chaos. Where in the world were they? The uncertainty I felt overwhelmed me as I grappled with three of Kübler-Ross's stages at one time: denial ('They can't be lost'), anger (at my boots), and bargaining ('Let me have my boots back and I promise I'll never be absent-minded again.')

Uncertainty can be overwhelming. In helping organizations manage expectations, I've found that uncertainty is one of the biggest grievances of both IT professionals and their customers, particularly in terms of not being kept informed about matters of importance. They wait for information that never comes. They watch for the e-mail reply to their query, and it never arrives. People refer to this situation as 'the black hole,' claiming that their request or problem must have fallen into the black hole because 'I never heard from them again.'

The absence of information people believe they should be receiving is a source of aggravation even in calm times. But when people are in chaos and expected information is not forthcoming, they imagine scenarios that are often much worse than the reality. And that's when rumors take hold.

As Nicholas DiFonzo explains in The *Watercooler Effect*, 'Waiting for news can actually be worse than receiving it – and people seize upon rumors in an attempt to end uncertainty.'[27]

Furthermore, people often see those who are not providing the information as deliberately – and even maliciously – withholding it. Even in a trusting relationship, people want to know what's happening and how it will affect them; not getting that information can eat away at trust.

> When people are in chaos and expected information is not forthcoming, they imagine scenarios that are often much worse than the reality.

To avoid this damaging outcome, it's wise periodically and proactively to offer information about the status of the change and what's in store for those affected. But don't assume that when you've offered this information once, you've done your job; updates at regular intervals can be crucial to people's acceptance of the change and their adjustment to it. In fact, for many people, the content of the updates is less important than the fact of the updates. Periodic communication about what's happening assures people that they haven't been forgotten.

By the way, my ski boots did reappear after having an experience of their own. (If you want the details, contact me at *naomi@nkarten.com*.)

---

[27] Nicholas DiFonzo, *The Watercooler Effect*, Avery, 2008, p. 84.

Communicate even in the absence of information

What if you're totally in favor of updating people regularly about the status of a change effort, but you have no new information to offer? Say, for example, that plans for a particular change have stalled since it was first announced. Or that senior management is working on next steps, but firm decisions in the short term are unlikely. The problem is that to people on the receiving end, the short term feels an awful lot like the long term.

In such situations, those who are driving the change effort know what's happening, even if all that's happening is the impatient twiddling of fingers. These finger-twiddlers may be frustrated by lack of progress, but at least it's frustration based on knowing what's happening (or not happening). Meanwhile, everyone else feels the much more debilitating frustration of not knowing, compounded by the fear of how the schemes they imagine are being hatched will affect them. People have no way of distinguishing information that's deliberately withheld from information they haven't received because there's nothing new to tell them.

The solution is simple: when a period of time has passed with no new information, explain that you have no new information to offer – and do so periodically. Emphasize that you know that they want to know what's happening and that you will provide more information when you can.

A situation that illustrated an effective way of handling the absence of information occurred when I was a passenger on a plane that was still at the gate after departure time. Very quickly, a flight attendant came on the loudspeaker and said that the plane had a mechanical problem and he didn't know how long it would take to fix. But, he told us, they'd give us an update every 15 minutes – and they'd give us that update every 15 minutes, even if they had nothing new to tell us.

Think about this situation:

1 They kept us informed, in contrast to the experiences we've all had on planes – and in the workplace – where something is going on and they tell us nothing.
2 They had a specific schedule for keeping us informed. And while planning how to announce a delay is a concession that delays might happen, it's better to accept that reality than be caught unprepared when it does happen.
3 They kept us informed even when there was no new information. That way, we wouldn't face a lengthy period of no updates, which would have fueled our angst and anger, and led us to see the airline as unconcerned and uncaring.
4 Most impressive of all, they informed us of their plans to keep us informed. They managed our expectations about how they were going to manage our expectations.

Taking this type of action gives people something to know, even if it's not what they were hoping to hear. In times of uncertainty, knowing something – anything – is better than knowing nothing at all.

Communicate about information you can't disclose

Here is one other aspect of giving people updates: suppose you have information about what's happening, but either you can't disclose it yet, or you aren't the one who can do the disclosing. This can happen, for example, when a company's financials will suffer if planned changes become public prematurely, or when management is unwilling to announce a change while several loose ends remain.

I faced a situation like this when I held a staff position reporting to Alec, a director. In my weekly meetings with Alec, he filled me in on all major matters. But I'd heard rumors about a possible budget freeze, and I wanted to know if it was true. When I asked Alec about it, he deflected my question with an impish grin and a change of subject. Finally, after a few weeks and several tries, I said to him, 'If you simply can't tell me, just tell me you can't tell me. You don't even have to give me a reason.' He said, 'I can't tell you.' And that was that.

Thereafter, we developed a signal, our own private wink and nod, for when he had information that I wanted but that he was not in a position to tell me. It spared me from repeatedly asking. It spared him from repeatedly changing the subject. It led both of us to appreciate the value of signals as a meaningful form of communication.

As education technology analyst, Pamela Livingston, notes, 'An honest "we're still working on this" goes a long way and is better than silence. People will respect leaders who respect them by treating them as professionals.' Of course, trust plays a key role here. If people see you as trustworthy, they'll accept your explanation because they know you play it straight. Otherwise, they'll view it as part of a pattern of obfuscation.

Explain the impact of a change on those affected

An example of how to leave people out of the loop during times of change occurred during a service-level agreement (SLA) effort. After extensive negotiation, the IT/customer

SLA team completed a comprehensive agreement. It was then that my client, Fred, an IT manager, made a huge mistake: he told his staff – the people who would have to deliver services that met the terms of the agreement – 'It's done, so live with it!'

Most of Fred's employees were unfamiliar with SLAs and knew nothing about how the agreement would affect their work. Fearing the worst – an unmanageable workload, long hours, unrelenting customer demands, humiliation if they couldn't meet the service levels agreed to – they were thrown into chaos. Morale plunged, taking productivity with it.

Fred failed to appreciate that everyone who would be accountable for the success of the SLA needed time to learn what was in it, how they'd benefit, and how it would affect their workload, responsibilities, priorities, and relationships. They needed information, education, and the feeling that someone – Fred, for example – understood what they were going through.

The organizations that are the most effective at easing people through the chaos associated with SLA-triggered change recognize that before making the agreement operational, they should explain the terms of the agreement to those who will be responsible for its success and invite their questions, concerns, and feedback.

This two-way communication – presenting information *to* affected personnel and soliciting information *from* them – helps them adjust to change. It's a valuable approach when the change involves a new methodology, tool, or business process, as Fred discovered when I asked him to hold off implementing the SLA and talk to his staff about what it meant for them. He reported back in amazement, 'They're OK with it now. That's all it took: communicating with them.'

Yes, sometimes, that's all it takes.

Invite people to contribute ideas about the change

People who are invited to offer input about a change tend to be more supportive of it than those who aren't – provided, of course, that their ideas are truly listened to and given a fair hearing. The opportunity to contribute is one of the steps that led to success in John Kotter and Holger Rathgeber's delightful fable about change, *Our Iceberg Is Melting.* This is the story of a colony of emperor penguins in Antarctica who faced a serious threat to their habitat.

As characters in a fable, these penguins could do things your average penguin can't, such as carry briefcases, hold meetings, adjust priorities, and, of course, resist change. Every one of the featured penguins reminds you of someone you've encountered at work, such as a penguin named NoNo, whose behavior needs no explanation.

It was not for nothing that Louis, the Head Penguin, was the penguin in charge. Louis saw that the challenge the colony faced would be better addressed by a team than by individual penguins acting unilaterally. As Kotter and Fathgeber explain, Louis took the 'difficult but essential step of pulling together a team to guide the needed change.'[28] In effect, Louis took the unprecedented step (unprecedented for penguins, at least) of empowering everyone to offer ideas and contribute to the effort.

Recall again the opening story in Chapter 1, in which Glenn sallied forth to carry out a company-wide upgrade. Imagine if, instead, he had invited several people from IT and customer departments to weigh in on his implementation plan. The result would have been a much better plan, one that would have avoided the devastating outcome that resulted.

Inviting people to have a say makes them feel valued. It generates valuable ideas, particularly from people who have a deeper understanding of how the change will affect their work than those leading the change. And it has the power to transform resistance into wholehearted support.

In times of change, people want to have a say. They want to be part of what's happening. All you have to do is let them.

---

[28] John Kotter and Holger Rathgeber, *Our Iceberg Is Melting*, St. Martin's Press, 2005, p. 55.

And, of course, take their input seriously, or they won't offer it next time around.

Give people a sense of control

During times of change, people often feel a lack of control and that feeling exacerbates the chaos they're in. Inviting them to have a say does something beyond making them feel valued and generating good ideas; it gives them a sense of control.

This need for control is not unique to situations of change. In an article about elevators, Nick Paumgarten notes that in most elevators built since the early 1990s, 'the door-close button doesn't work. It is there mainly to make you think it works.' In other words, it gives passengers a sense of control. He adds that once you're aware of this, 'it can be illuminating to watch people compulsively press the door-close button. That the door eventually closes reinforces their belief in the button's power.'[29] Even having read this article, I remain convinced that my button-pushing causes the door to close sooner than it would otherwise!

> The lack of control people feel during times of change exacerbates the chaos they're in.

This feeling of a lack of control might sound like a petty reaction to not getting one's way, but it's not. In *Stumbling on Happiness*, Harvard psychology professor, Daniel Gilbert, points out that

[29] Nick Paumgarten, 'Up and Then Down,' *New Yorker*, 21 April 2008, p. 6.

Being effective – changing things, influencing things, making things happen – is one of the fundamental needs with which human brains seem to be naturally endowed, and much of our behavior from infancy onward is simply an expression of this penchant for control.

He adds that research suggests that if people lose their ability to control things, 'they become unhappy, helpless, hopeless, and depressed.'[30]

Recall the overview of Kübler-Ross's stages of grief in Chapter 2 – patients fared better when they controlled a minor matter like deciding when they would see visitors. But the matter of giving control is more complex than it appears at first, as Gilbert reports in describing a study that had shocking results. In the study, researchers arranged for student volunteers to periodically visit nursing-home residents. A high-control group of residents had control over the timing and duration of these visits. A low-control group had no say in the matter. After several months, the high-control group was healthier, happier, and more active than the low-control group.

Then came the shocker. When the study ended, so did the visits. Several months later, a disproportionate number of residents in the high-control group had died.

In this study, gaining control improved well-being. Losing that control seriously damaged it. Change in the workplace normally doesn't have life-or-death consequences. But at work, just as in these research studies, people in chaos often grasp at anything that confers a scrap of control – or even the appearance of control.

---

[30] Daniel Gilbert, *Stumbling on Happiness*, Alfred A. Knopf, 2006, pp. 20–1.

As Gilbert reports, 'Our desire to control is so powerful, and the feeling of being in control so rewarding, that people often act as though they can control the uncontrollable.'[31]

The feeling of a loss of control feeds on itself and prevents access to a solution. Furthermore, as consultant and psychotherapist, Jean McLendon, points out, 'The physical reaction to losing control, such as clamping down or tightening up, interferes with dealing with the situation that provoked the reaction.'[32] For some people, resistance is their way of exerting control, when they otherwise feel they have none at all.

Creating teams to offer recommendations about a change may seem like a nuisance and a distraction, and sometimes it is. The same is true of inviting people to have some say about a change. But the payoff is likely to be faster and less grudging acceptance of the change by those who might otherwise stall progress, or just take longer to reach a new status quo.

Help people understand each other's perspectives

Relationships that fall apart are a form of unplanned change that can trigger extreme chaos. I saw an excellent example of this when I was contacted by Jack, an IT vice president, who described four departments that had to interact with each other on behalf of customers. But relationships among the departments had dwindled badly, damaging their responsiveness to each other and to their customers.

---

[31] Ibid., p. 22.

[32] Jean McLendon, Satir coaching session, Amplifying Your Effectiveness Conference, 6 November 2007.

As I listened to Jack describe the situation, I realized that each of the departments had become a foreign element to the other three, and the result was a state of mass chaos. This was chaos brought about not by change foisted on them from outside, but rather by a change in relationships that had once been smooth.

By the time Jack called me, he was frantic, explaining, 'They're about to kill each other. Can you help?'

Jack wanted me to help kill them? Well, no, of course not. He wanted me to help defuse the tension among the four groups and restore their ability to work together. When we gathered in a hotel meeting room (the better, I assume, to spare company property if a fight broke out), it was immediately obvious that many in each department had never even met those in the other departments. To each other, they were voices on the phone and messages in an inbox. This situation is common in dispersed teams, but these people worked in the same building.

I invited them to divide into four groups, one group per department, to discuss some topics designed to help them see that, despite their wranglings with each other, they all basically wanted the same things.

And indeed, when they reported out after their discussions, it was clear that everyone wanted to do good work. Everyone wanted to deliver high-quality service to their customers. Everyone wanted to be treated with respect. For the first time, they had the opportunity to see how much they had in common.

Through a series of activities, the group came to understand that each department faced pressures and priorities that weren't obvious to the others. Thus enlightened, they quickly discovered solutions to some of the technical problems they'd been having in working together.

As a final activity, I had them form small groups in which every group included people from all four departments. I asked them to discuss where they wanted to go from here in terms of their relationships with each other. In no time at all, they identified numerous ways they could continue the discussions they'd now begun.

These departments still had plenty to do to work effectively with each other; their processes and particularly their handoffs needed attention. But with the chaos among them diminished and their newfound willingness to talk to each other and listen to each other, they were able to focus on these improvements.

Food for thought

1 Which of the suggestions in this chapter have you seen handled well in recent changes? Which ones have been handled poorly?

2 In the next change that you lead, which of these suggestions do you want to pay particular attention to?

3 In what ways can you give those affected by a change a greater sense of control? What would give you a greater sense of control when you're the one affected by the change?

4 What other aspects of talking to the people affected by change would you recommend?

CHAPTER 10: OFFERING CARING COMMUNICATION

This chapter adds to Chapter 9 by offering the following suggestions for caring communication and communicating with care:

1 Focus on thoughts, feelings, and needs.
2 Speak of the old way with respect.
3 Recognize the power of empathy.
4 Listen persuasively.
5 Monitor your choice of voice.
6 Offer encouragement.
7 Use humor – judiciously.
8 Acknowledge success and progress.

Focus on thoughts, feelings, and needs

When you meet with subordinates and others to inquire how well they're handling the change, be careful with your wording. The reason is that some people are more oriented toward thinking and others are more oriented toward feeling, and the words you use will influence their reaction to your inquiry and therefore their response.

Some people both in and outside of IT don't like to acknowledge having feelings and prefer to rely on what their head tells them. As psychology professor, Daniel Gilbert, describes in *Stumbling on Happiness*, 'Some people seem to be keenly aware of their moods and feelings, and may even have a novelist's gift for describing their every shade and flavor.'[33] Others, he explains, have a more basic emotional vocabulary. And some people lack the words to describe emotional states, a syndrome that apparently occurs often enough to have a name: alexithymia. Talking with people who are thinking-oriented about their feelings may generate a negative response, unless you first inquire about, and acknowledge, their thoughts and ideas.

Just the opposite is true, of course, of people who rely on feelings to guide them. These are people who know their feelings and trust them, and it's important for anyone who talks with them to appreciate and respect this orientation and to communicate accordingly. Talking with feelings-oriented people about their thoughts and ideas may prove to be counterproductive, unless you first inquire about, and acknowledge, their feelings.

The challenge is that you can't necessarily know whether those facing change are more oriented toward thinking or toward feeling. And if it's an entire group that's affected, it is likely to include some of each.

Therefore, if you want to solicit their input or find out how they're doing, one approach is to ask in a way that acknowledges both perspectives, such as, 'What are your thoughts and feelings about the way we're handling this?' Or use neutral terminology that doesn't favor either perspective, such as, 'How are you doing with this change?' or 'What's happening for you in adjusting to this change?'

In any case, in asking others how they're doing, you might generate more useful information by asking work-specific

---

[33] Daniel Gilbert, *Stumbling on Happiness*, Alfred A. Knopf, 2006, p. 62.

questions that will give you insight into how to help them move to a new status quo. Consider, for example:

1. How are you doing with this new process (or development method, or whatever)?
2. What's working well for you?
3. What are you finding confusing or puzzling?
4. What concerns do you have?
5. What difficulties are you facing?
6. What one or two things would most help you move forward?

These questions are action-oriented. They help you know what's going on with these people and they give you an idea of what you need to do – or help them do – to move forward.

Speak of the old way with respect

I recently read an article by a consultant who claimed that the fastest way to implement change is to disparage what people are being asked to give up. This is spectacularly bad advice.

People become attached to the ways they do things; those ways become part of their very identity. Even when they find those ways tedious or burdensome, they know what to do and what to expect. As a result, people often prefer the old status quo, even when they positively hate it. Therefore, belittling the old way in hopes of generating enthusiasm about the new way is likely to trigger resentment and slow down acceptance of the change.

I once experienced this reaction at first hand in a company in which top management decided to switch to a new mainframe platform. Not one of us was happy with this decision. We were used to the current platform. We viewed it as vastly superior. Besides, it was the industry standard, and we feared we'd have a tough time finding qualified staff.

At a presentation to introduce us to the new platform, the vendor representative repeatedly touted the superiority of his platform and bashed ours. Clearly unschooled in the art of managing change, he responded to every question with disparaging remarks about our current platform. Rather than recognizing that we were dealing with the loss of something important to us and conceding that our current mainframe was not entirely worthless, he turned every question into an adversarial situation.

People in chaos are far more focused on the pain of what they're losing than on the benefits of what they're gaining. Although it's fine to tout the benefits of the new way, don't do it in a way that discredits or shows a lack of respect for the old way.

In fact, do just the opposite: acknowledge what people are being asked to give up and the role it has played in their lives. If possible, identify similarities between the old and the new – this helps people see that while much is changing, some things will remain the same. People are unlikely to jump with joy at the similarities, but they'll be less likely to feel stomped on if they don't have to contend with disrespectful remarks from representatives of the New Way.

> Acknowledge what people are being asked to give up and the role it has played in their lives.

Recognize the power of empathy

Empathy can reduce the duration and intensity of chaos. In fact, it's one of the most important communication tools for managing chaos.

Of course, some people excel at *not* expressing empathy, as Lou Russell, co-author of *IT Leadership Alchemy*, discovered at a hotel she was staying at. In the morning, just out of the shower, she turned on the hairdryer and out came ... a flame! Fortunately, she wasn't pointing the hairdryer at herself at that moment and wasn't hurt. She immediately called the front desk to report the situation. The conversation, as she described it to me, went something like this:

> Lou: 'I just turned on the hairdryer and a flame came shooting out.'
>
> Front-desk person: 'Well, we don't have any more hairdryers right now, so you'll have to make do.'

We can come up with all sorts of reasons for this bizarre response, from cluelessness to inexperience to fear of hotel liability if she had acknowledged the presence of a fire-breathing hairdryer. Whatever the explanation, this is a precious example of how not to show empathy.

Expressing empathy during times of change is about communicating with concern for the chaos people are experiencing. That's the lesson learned by a facilities team that was responsible for arranging the relocation of individuals, teams, departments, and entire divisions. Some of the relocations were to the other side of the floor; some were to the other side of the country. Given the complexity of the technology involved, IT was their toughest client.

People form strong emotional attachments to their home and work space, and moving somewhere else can be chaos-provoking. Because of this, the facilities team had a tough job; the moves they arranged were mandated, yet their clients in IT and other divisions were forced to disrupt work that didn't allow for time-outs.

When I presented the Satir change model to help the team understand their clients' perspective, they saw how they could use the power of empathy to reduce their clients' stress and, in the process, their own.

In particular, they decided to contact their clients further in advance of a planned move and to follow up periodically as the date of the move approached. In addition, they started sending out friendly reminders about often-overlooked details. Realizing that empathic listening was one of the most important things they could do, they started giving their clients an opportunity to express their grievances about an upcoming move.

The facilities team astutely realized that supporting the needs of people who are in chaos threw them into chaos as well. To address their own chaos, they resolved to refrain from taking their clients' complaints personally and instead to acknowledge their client's anxieties. They discovered that empathic attention diminished their clients' chaos – and their own as well.

If expressions of empathy don't come easily to you, notice those times when you *are* being empathic. Take note of what you say and how you say it, and adapt those instances to the situations you face at work. Sometimes something as simple as 'I'm sorry to hear that' will suffice. Or 'I have a feeling you're really busy right now,' or 'I understand how important this is for you.'

Or (in the case of fire-breathing hairdryers in hotels), 'Are you OK?'

Listen persuasively

I once came across a greeting card that said, 'What most people really need ... [and on the inside] is a good listening to.' How true. Most people are so preoccupied with their own priorities and pressures that they rarely take the time to listen – *really* listen – to others. The failure to listen can trigger disillusionment, a drop in morale, and a 'why-even-bother?' attitude in those who feel they're not being listened to. And this reaction is all the more intense when people are in the throes of chaos.

Unfortunately, many people do a poor job of listening. Being a good listener means more than just switching your ears into the 'on' position; it means looking like you're listening. I call this 'persuasive listening': listening so that it's clear to the person speaking to you that you're fully present, focused on them, and truly hearing what they're saying.

Do not underestimate the power of listening as a tool for managing change. In my consulting work, I sometimes hold one-on-one sessions with IT employees and their business counterparts. For many of them, the opportunity to sound off to someone who listens attentively is cathartic. Even as they acknowledge that their grousing won't change anything, many thank me for the opportunity to say what's on their minds. 'I feel better now,' they tell me.

Do not underestimate the power of listening as a tool for managing change.

Keep the greeting card in mind: often what people want more than anything else is to know that those in charge appreciate what they're going through. Therefore, make sure you give the person who's speaking your full attention, and respond in a way that focuses on the person and stays on the topic.

Monitor your choice of voice

Most of the time, we have control over our tone of voice. But in times of stress, such as that experienced during change, people sometimes speak in a way that conveys an intention or an attitude other than the one they intended. Take 'Are you OK?' (the words not spoken by a certain hotel staff person) as an example. Imagine how you might say it if you wanted to express frustration. Or impatience. Or condescension. Your voice takes on a certain tone, and that tone – plus the facial expression that accompanies it when you're face to face – can exacerbate the chaos people are experiencing.

When I think of how the slightest modulation of one's voice can change one's implied intention, I'm reminded of tonal languages. For example, in Mandarin Chinese, a single syllable can be spoken with a flat tone, a low-to-high tone, a high-to-low tone and a high-to-low-to-high tone.

When I took a class in Mandarin Chinese, I learned that depending on which tone you use, the syllable *ma* can mean 'mother,' 'hemp,' 'horse,' or 'scold,' hardly trivial differences. The syllable *yi* (pronounced 'ee') can mean 'move,' 'chair,' 'one' or (believe it or not) 'hundred million.' Even more amazing, the words for 'buy' and 'sell' differ only in the tone used.

Although English is not a tonal language, speakers of English are very good at applying different intonations to even the briefest utterances to convey different attitudes and intentions. Indeed, children can do this as soon as they learn to talk.

And as adults? Think about the multitude of different ways you can say 'no,' so that each version conveys a different message. Managers who want to ease the stress of change, will pay attention to their tone of voice and make adjustments to that tone when needed.

Offer encouragement

Encouragement, sincerely offered, can help people move more expeditiously through the change cycle. People who are in chaos may be especially in need of encouragement to alleviate their fears, uncertainty, perceived loss of control, and difficulty accomplishing what is now expected of them.

Encouragement is also valuable when people are moving into the practice and integration stage, a time of adjustment that's more likely to be a bumpy ride than a smooth transition to the new status quo. People are learning new ways. Learning inevitably entails functioning more slowly than usual and making mistakes until the new way becomes familiar. In the process, people may seem to be making progress, then slip back, repeating mistakes they had successfully overcome.

The very experience of stumbling can toss people back into chaos. You can help people during this stage by not being unduly hard on them when they slip back. Encourage them to remember that this sliding back is a normal part of the adjustment. Let them know that you know they're in a period of adjustment. While certainly not welcoming a dip in productivity and the associated errors and delays, you can reassure people that this is an inevitable part of any adjustment process.

The fact that this stage is often one of alternatively making progress and slipping back doesn't mean you should accept an intolerable level of blunders. Still, encouragement – in the form of education, support, and perhaps handholding – can help to abbreviate this period of adjustment.

In working with IT clients who are making the transition to agile methods, Ellen Gottesdiener, author of *Requirements by Collaboration*, encourages people to experiment. As she points out, the transition to agile methods is really a change effort. The fear of making a mistake, or getting stuck, stifles people's willingness to try something different. To help them get past their anxiety and skepticism, she reassures them by giving them an assignment and telling them, 'It's just an experiment.' And it works, helping them feel safe as they figure out how to do what initially seemed undoable.

Use humor – judiciously

Humor can be a survival tool during stressful times. But people in chaos are not always as receptive to humor as they might otherwise be. Furthermore, they may view attempts at humor by others as belittling what they're going through. Therefore, it's best to use humor cautiously, keeping in mind what you know about the people involved and what they seem able to tolerate.

Still, humor is sometimes exactly what's needed to reduce the chaos. When I was a client support manager, I used a lighthearted approach to help my staff cope with our demanding customers, critical deadlines, and the mistakes that sometimes occurred in the rush to be responsive. A few days before year-end, I bought some bright blue stickers in two sizes, medium and large. I wrote the name of each person in the department on two medium-sized stickers and one large sticker.

I called my staff together and told them I wanted give them something special for the coming year. I then gave them each the three stickers with their name on it. I explained that these stickers entitled each of them to two medium-sized screw-ups and one totally outrageous screw-up during the next year without fear of repercussions.

In my best mock-serious voice, I explained, 'If you turn in the appropriate sticker at the time of the screw-up, I'll let you off the hook, provided you follow these six rules.'

I then advised them of the rules:

1 To be let off the hook, you must turn the sticker in at the time of the screw-up.
2 Two medium-sized stickers are equivalent to one large sticker, entitling you to two totally outrageous screw-ups rather than one outrageous screw-up and two medium-sized ones.
3 Any problem I don't know about won't be held against you. However, if you withhold information about a serious problem and I learn about it anyway, you'll forfeit all your stickers, and possibly much more.
4 If a screw-up results from the combined effort of two or more of you, you can each turn in half a sticker. Fractions less than one-half will not be accepted.
5 Minor screw-ups should just be fixed without any special fanfare.
6 At the end of next year, all unused stickers will become null and void, so there is no point exhibiting a year's worth of exemplary behavior in hopes of retaining stickers for the following year.

They got the point: chaos was our status quo and problems would occur. When they did, our approach would be to acknowledge them, accept responsibility, resolve them, and learn from them. We all agreed that having an environment in which we could laugh at ourselves and with each other would help us maintain our sanity during times of chaos.

This type of 'sticker strategy' doesn't work with people who take themselves too seriously. Fortunately, we didn't suffer from that affliction.

Acknowledge success and progress

When I had knee surgery, my recovery took forever, or so it seemed. At first, just walking across the living room took the better part of forever. I may have walked a little further each day, but I barely noticed my progress from one day to the next. Once I was fully recovered, I was able to look back and see the enormous progress I'd made.

I found this experience to be a striking example of adjustment to change: it's much easier to recognize one's adjustment to change in looking back over a stretch of time than to see it from one day to the next. When people are in the practice and integration stage, each day looks and feels much like the preceding one, and they may be oblivious to the progress they're making.

For that reason, astute managers acknowledge even small successes and call attention to progress that people may not appreciate they're making. Some managers like to hold celebrations at key milestones to acknowledge progress. Other methods include personal notes of recognition, mementos, hearty kudos, or wall charts that display progress. In some groups, even just a reminder at a monthly meeting to 'look how far we've come' will work.

It's especially uplifting when it's the customers who tout IT's progress – all the more so when it's the customers you least expect to do so. In a company for which I did SLA consulting, service delivery improved dramatically over the course of a year. But recollections of the sorry service of a year earlier were still fresh in the minds of many customers. At a joint IT–customer meeting on the first anniversary of the SLA, a customer vice president who had been highly cynical about IT's abilities posted a chart of improvements his departments had experienced due to IT's efforts. He urged his staff to notice and appreciate the progress that had taken place.

Indeed, IT professionals and their customers can help one another by each observing and commenting on progress made possible through the efforts of the other.

It can also be valuable to reflect on progress from the longer vantage point of several years, as was the case at a company in which morale plunged during a monumental merger. Several years later, I visited the company and met with some of the people who had survived the merger.

When I described the Satir change model and asked how things were now, one fellow said that, as impossible as it had seemed when the merger first occurred, they had indeed achieved a new status quo. He said there were still some loose ends from the merger, but none that caused the same level of chaos as the initial transition.

Several people in this group also said that the change turned out to be for the better in ways that they couldn't have anticipated initially – a common reaction in looking back.

Food for thought

1 How do you rate yourself in terms of the suggestions in this chapter? What have you done well? What could use some improvement?

2 In the next change that you lead, which of these suggestions do you want to pay particular attention to?

3 Think of a situation in which those leading a change spoke in a disparaging manner about the old way. What effect did this have on the change effort?

4 What advice would you offer others about the role of listening and empathy during times of change?

CHAPTER 11: LEARNING FROM THE EXPERIENCE OF CHANGE

Faced with change, employees have one question: 'What's going to happen to me?' A successful change management communication program will avoid that question.

Scott Adams, *The Dilbert Principle*[34]

Numerous colleagues who work in and with IT have told me about change efforts characterized by a serious disregard for the people affected. In a striking number of change efforts, people were given no rationale for the change, no information about the goal, no idea about what would happen and when, no clue as to how it would affect their work, and little support to ease the transition.

The words my colleagues used in describing the experience of those affected have included 'apathy,' 'sadness,' 'burdened,' 'betrayed,' 'unmotivated,' 'miserable,' and 'depressed.'

It needn't be this way.

In the best of cases, major change is difficult. What better reason is there to strive to minimize the duration and the intensity of the chaos associated with the change? This chapter concludes this book with the following suggestions:

1 Learn from the successes of others.

2 Help people understand that they will adjust.

3 Make the new status quo a time of reflection.

4 Educate people about the experience of change.

---

[34] Scott Adams, *The Dilbert Principle*, HarperBusiness, 1996, p. 199.

5 Avoid the biggest mistake managers make.

Learn from the successes of others

Every change effort I've witnessed or learned about that reached a new status quo with a minimum of chaos, displayed sensitivity to the people affected and thoughtful, concerned communication. Here are three examples.

Example 1: Smoothing the way for workers

Debbie Exner, a business and personal coach, described a banking client she had during her earlier career helping companies implement new technology. The bank was rolling out a new credit card system to replace a half-dozen systems that were text-based and chock-full of cryptic codes. Experienced workers had all the codes memorized and were very comfortable bouncing around among the different systems, but this hodgepodge of systems was a training nightmare for new hires.

The new system was thoroughly modern, with a graphical user interface, drop-down menus, and a consistent look and feel – and it was as different as could be from the previous systems, a situation that could easily have generated resistance and complaints. But it didn't because, as Exner reports, 'The client went to great efforts to smooth the way with kickoff meetings, giveaway campaigns to build excitement for the new system, and lots of training that focused on the benefits of the new system.'

Due to these up-front efforts in anticipating and tending to worker needs, acceptance of the new system was quite high.

Example 2: Communication as a priority

Education technology analyst, Pamela Livingston, told me about the emphasis placed on communication during the implementation of a new e-mail system. Communicating in multiple ways was a priority and included making announcements during a faculty meeting, describing the new system in a newsletter, and putting flyers about it in mailboxes.

But that's not all. The people driving the change reached out personally to everyone at the school, dropping by to mention it, asking if there were questions, talking about it in the faculty room, and having the tech support staff mention it. The tech support staff passed along what they knew when troubleshooting issues arose. According to Livingston, the new system was accepted quickly.

Example 3: Creating a communication plan

Isabel Fenichel-Berg, a human resources vice president, described an outsourcing initiative at a previous company that resulted in a staff reduction of 85 people. This kind of transition can be difficult for everyone involved. In some companies, it's downright traumatic.

Not so in Fenichel-Berg's company. At the heart of what made the undertaking successful was a carefully planned communication program. Meetings were held for the entire staff to explain the business rationale. Everyone was given a thorough understanding of the process, from inception to implementation, including a specific timeline.

The people whose jobs were affected were given some interviewing guidance and were then interviewed by the outsourcing vendor for open positions. Of the 85 people, 70 were hired by the vendor and were able to continue delivering services to the company. The remaining 15 were given incentives to stay with the company until the final transition and then released with severance packages that were linked to their years of service.

Yes, people were nervous about what would transpire, but that nervousness was minimized because people knew what was going to happen. They knew what to expect. They didn't have to fear that information was being kept from them, because it wasn't.

When the transition was over, those who remained were eager to continue in their roles. And those who'd been released didn't have to recover from a thrashing to their confidence and self-esteem, because they understood that the terminations were due to downsizing and were not a function of their performance.

Do people matter during a change effort? Yes, indeed, they do. And does thoughtful communication during change efforts lead to a better result? Absolutely!

Help people understand that they *will* adjust

When a change effort is in full swing, and people are facing a distaste for the new way, it's difficult for them to imagine that they'll ever come to terms with it. Sometimes, though, the new status quo isn't as far away as it might have initially seemed. And often, it holds pleasant surprises.

Sometimes, the new status quo isn't as far away as it might initially seem. And often, it holds pleasant surprises.

Here's an example: Sandy, a woman in one of my seminars, described how upset she had been three years earlier, when, due to overcrowding, her department was relocated to a building miles from the headquarters campus.

The announcement that the department was being moved plunged Sandy into chaos. She didn't want any part of the new location. She detested being off-site and away from the familiar goings-on. She hated being away from her friends in other departments. She resented being out of the loop.

So what happened? She adjusted, and so did the others in her department. To their surprise, they discovered several benefits to their new location. For one, they had an easier commute and didn't have to compete for parking spaces. And sure, they missed the action at her former location, but now they had room to spread out and peace and quiet to do their jobs.

Best of all, she said, they could now raise their voices if they wanted to, even shout across the room if they felt like it, knowing they wouldn't be disturbing coworkers in other departments. This was *their* space in a way that their previous work location hadn't been, and they loved it.

The adjustment was gradual, and, not anticipating it, they didn't notice it happening. Proof that they had adjusted came two years later when they were told that due to an expansion at headquarters, they were now to move back. And they didn't want to go. They liked their quiet, peaceful, convenient, off-site location and hated the idea of returning.

When people are in the midst of chaos and looking toward an uncertain future, it's hard to imagine that any benefit at all will emerge. And of course, not every change is to a better place. But so often, the new status quo has benefits and opportunities that are not foreseeable when you're deep in chaos; they become evident only later on.

When you are managing a team that is in chaos, remind them of other transitions they've made in which the future looked bleak, but proved to be anything but.

Make new status quo a time of reflection

I have to believe that when my cat, Pooky, slithered out the window of our eighth-floor apartment many years ago and fell to the sidewalk, she felt a touch of chaos. So did we when we found her scratch marks on the ledge outside the window that we'd always kept closed (except for this one time!). Amazingly, neither her descent nor her landing did her any harm. Without a moment's reflection about what she had learned from this fall, she went on to fully enjoy her eight remaining chaos-filled lives.

In *Stumbling on Happiness*, Professor Daniel Gilbert states that even though nonhuman animals act at times as though they think about the future, humans think about the future in a way that no other animal can or does. He claims, amusingly, that he'll stick to this view until 'a chimp weeps at the thought of growing old alone, or smiles as it contemplates its summer vacation, or turns down a Fudgsicle because it already looks too fat in shorts.'[35]

For us humans, the memory of a bout of chaos and how we coped with it can influence our reaction to potential future occurrences. For some people, in fact, the fear of future chaos can itself be a foreign element resulting in even more

[35] Daniel Gilbert, *Stumbling on Happiness*, Alfred A. Knopf, 2006, p. 4.

chaos. But we have the advantage over falling felines because we can learn from the experience of chaos and apply what we've learned to future change efforts.

One of the best ways to learn from chaos – and from the entire experience of change – is to do so deliberately by using the relative serenity of the new status quo as a time for reflection.

Granted, whether you work in or with IT, you have more than enough to keep you busy. Perhaps, though, you're on a project team that has learned the value of conducting a post-project retrospective to formally examine what you did well, what you learned, what confused you, and what you want to do the same or differently in the next project. These are the kinds of issues that, left unexamined, are easily forgotten by the start of the next project. Retrospectives provide a way to look at a project from multiple perspectives and gain insight into aspects of it that didn't make sense at the time.

Because of its many benefits, retrospectives can also be valuable at the end of a change effort as a formal process of learning from the experience. Of course, the timing of a change retrospective may be fuzzier than with a project. Projects have (at least in theory) a clear end-point. But the end of a change effort is the achievement of a new status quo, a time or situation without clear markers. Therefore, if you're leading a change, or guiding a team through a change driven by others, it's your job to select an appropriate point from which to take a look back.

Conducting a change retrospective can help you improve the way you handle changes that, at one time, would have propelled you into chaos. An example is an IT manager I met, who, over a period of years, worked at several different companies, each of which eventually merged with another company. The first such merger was chaos personified. But from each merger, she explicitly drew lessons that enabled her to use her merger know-how as a competitive advantage in her career, enabling her to rise quickly.

The learning process is one that any group can experience. Management consultant, Steve Smith, emphasizes this point, noting that after many change cycles, groups

> become learning organizations – they learn how to cope with change. The members of these organizations are not threatened or anxious about the types of situations that they used to experience as foreign elements. Instead, these situations excite and motivate them.[36]

But, with reflection, you can learn more and learn it faster than working through one change cycle and then another and another.

Questions for retrospectives

In conducting a retrospective for a given change effort or change experience, a team might discuss such questions as:

1 How would we describe the experience?

[36] Steven M. Smith, 'The Satir Change Model,' available at *www.stevenmsmith.com/my-articles/article/the-satir-change-model.html*.

2 How do our descriptions differ from each other and what do such differences tell us?
3 What did we do well in adapting to the change?
4 What didn't we do so well?
5 What was chaos like for us?
6 What surprised us?
7 What troubled us?
8 What did we learn?
9 What mysteries remain?
10 Based on this experience, what will we do differently next time?

You can count on the fact that people will vary in how they view the change effort and therefore in how they respond to the above questions.

In addition, here are some questions based on the Satir change model that you can reflect on privately or as part of a change retrospective:

1 How did your experience with this change map onto the Satir model?
2 What aspects of the change were foreign elements for you?
3 How did you respond to these foreign elements?
4 When you were in chaos, what happened to your mental state? What about your emotional stability? What might others have noticed when you were in chaos?
5 What did you notice about other people facing the same change?
6 What helped or hindered your ability to move out of chaos?

7 What were some sources of transforming ideas for you?
8 Based on the above, what can you do differently in the future, individually and as a team, to improve the way you handle change?
9 What do you want to keep in mind in the future in helping others cope with chaos?

Mini-retrospectives

It seems a shame to wait until the end of a project to make adjustments, clarify confusion, or repair misunderstandings that could have been addressed during the course of the project – if only you'd been aware of the need. Project mini-retrospectives can be conducted at milestones or intervals during a project to identify and address such concerns.

Mini-retrospectives for change efforts are similar and entail taking time to reflect on your reactions as the foreign element strikes, as you traverse the bumpy terrain of chaos, and as you find your way to a new status quo. Consider taking a time-out during your change efforts to look at how it's going and how you're doing. I guarantee, you'll come up with insights that you would have missed otherwise, and that might help speed your progress toward a new status quo.

Educate people about the experience of change

In *Becoming a Technical Leader*, Jerry Weinberg points out that one of the problems in implementing change is that 'when change doesn't fit our model, we try to stop it from happening.'[37] Educating people about the change cycle can improve their understanding of change and, therefore, the way they manage and cope with it. I encourage you to present the Satir change model (or any other change model that appeals to you) to your coworkers, peers, and others.

Whenever I've presented the Satir model, people have come to appreciate that change is a process that takes place over time, and, even if they feel unsettled right now, they will eventually achieve a new normal. Especially important, they come to recognize that the uncomfortable feeling they have during change has a name – chaos – and that chaos is normal. Discussions during these presentations regularly elicit comments like 'That's exactly what I went through,' and 'That explains why I could barely even function.'

Once people see previous changes in terms of the model, you can have them reflect on what they're currently experiencing and how it is similar to, or different from, past changes. Ask them what the model suggests about things they can do to adjust to the change more expeditiously. Having the model as a focal point helps them see their experience as part of a cycle of adjustment, and one they're actually already familiar with.

In fact, one group I worked with posted a depiction of the model in their work area, and every morning members of the group each placed a sticky note with their initials on it on the place on the model that represented where they were that day. This visual approach gave everyone in the group an instant take on how the group was faring.

---

[37] Gerald M. Weinberg, *Becoming a Technical Leader*, Dorset House Publishing, 1986, p. 11.

One of the most valuable aspects of the Satir change model is its terminology. People quickly grasp the notion of foreign elements, chaos, and so on. These terms become a shared language that enables them to discuss what they're experiencing in a new and helpful way.

Avoid the biggest mistake managers make

As Lou Russell and Jeff Feldman note in *IT Leadership Alchemy*, 'While the choice to change may be determined at the speed of management decision making, the unfolding of change takes place at people speed.'[38] This reminder applies to those working both in and with IT.

Therefore, take care to avoid the biggest mistake that managers make in implementing change: introducing the change and expecting people to embrace it and adjust to it instantly and with no impact on productivity – a leap from foreign element directly to new status quo. Managers who view it this way overlook, ignore, or are just plain oblivious to the messy, yet inevitable, intervening stage of chaos.

> Avoid the biggest mistake that managers make in implementing change: introducing the change and expecting people to embrace it instantly.

[38] Lou Russell and Jeff Feldman, *IT Leadership Alchemy*, Prentice Hall PTR, 2003, p. 216.

Don't make this mistake. Think about how people are likely to react. For example:

1. Think about how best to inform people about the change: who is the best person to communicate the information? Who already has the trust and confidence of the people who need to be informed? If appropriate, identify someone from among those affected by the change to help in introducing the change.
2. Consider what kinds of information people are likely to want or need. Some will want facts and information: a plan, a schedule, a set of events. Some will want to grasp the impact on them and others they care about. Many will want to know how they'll be kept informed about what's transpiring.
3. Think about which individuals or groups can support the change effort as it proceeds. Consider different ways that information about the status of the change can be made available so people have a sense of where things stand.
4. Help people understand the unsettling experience of chaos. Remember the importance of information, empathy, reassurance, encouragement, and feedback in helping people make their way through chaos to a new status quo.
5. Be patient as people adjust to change. This is one of the biggest challenges in leading a change effort – and the mark of a skilled change leader.
6. Show respect and consideration for the people affected by a change. The result will be a smoother trip to the new status quo for them and for you as well.

Finally, keep in mind that if, as a result of this book, you will be changing the way you manage and communicate change, then some of the ideas I've offered may be foreign elements that throw *you* into chaos when you try to apply them. If that happens, recognize that you are traveling through the change cycle. Think about what will help you minimize the duration and the intensity of your chaos. Expect to make mistakes as you proceed through the practice and integration stage. When you reach a new status quo, reflect on what you learned from the experience. And enjoy the journey!

Final food for thought

1 How will you make sure you learn from the changes you will inevitably experience?

2 What might you do to help those you work with learn from their change experiences?

Contact me

In this book, I've tried to offer ideas that will help you take a human-centered approach to change, with emphasis on communication as a tool for minimizing the duration and intensity of the chaos associated with change.

Please visit my website, *www.nkarten.com*, for articles on managing change and many related topics, as well as for information on my presentations and workshops on these topics.

I'd enjoy hearing from you. Feel free to contact me any time at *naomi@nkarten.com*. We can share our experiences, compare our perspectives, and have a few laughs at the craziness of it all. I look forward to hearing from you.

BIBLIOGRAPHY

The following list includes all the books and articles I've cited, as well as others on related topics.

Scott Adams, *The Dilbert Principle: A Cubicle's-Eye View of Bosses, Meetings, Management Fads & Other Workplace Afflictions*, HarperBusiness, 1996, ISBN 978-0-887308-58-1

William Bridges, *Managing Transitions: Making the Most of Change*, Perseus Books, 1991, ISBN 0-201-55073-3

Stephen M. R. Covey, *The Speed of Trust: The One Thing That Changes* Everything, Free Trust, 2006, ISBN 978-0-743297-30-1

Nicholas DiFonzo, *The Watercooler Effect: A Psychologist Explores the Extraordinary Power of Rumors*, Avery, 2008, ISBN 978-1-583333-25-9

Jeanie Daniel Duck, *The Change Monster: The Human Forces That Fuel or Foil Corporate Transformation & Change*, Three Rivers Press, 2001, ISBN 978-0-609808-81-8

Jutta Eckstein, *Agile Software Development in the Large: Diving into the Deep*, Dorset House Publishing, 2004, ISBN 978-0-932633-57-6

Daniel Gilbert, *Stumbling on Happiness*, Alfred A. Knopf, 2006, ISBN 978-1-400077-42-7

Ellen Gottesdiener, *Requirements by Collaboration: Workshops for Defining Needs*, Addison-Wesley, 2002, ISBN 978-0-201786-06-4

Payson Hall, 'Tending Communication Paths,' in *Better Software Magazine*, October 2007

Sandra Krebs Hirsh, with Jane A. G. Kise, *Work It Out: Clues for Solving People Problems at Work*, Davies-Black Publishing, 1996, ISBN 978-0-891060-88-8

Naomi Karten, *Communication Gaps and How to Close Them*, Dorset House Publishing, 2002, ISBN 978-0-932633-53-8

Naomi Karten, *How to Establish Service Level Agreements*, Karten Associates, 2003

Naomi Karten, *How to Survive, Excel and Advance as an Introvert*, Karten Associates, 2006

Naomi Karten, *Managing Expectations: Working with People Who Want More, Better, Faster, Sooner, NOW!*, Dorset House Publishing, 1994, ISBN 978-0-932633-27-9

Naomi Karten, *Perceptions & Realities* newsletter, posted for downloading at http://www.nkarten.com/newslet.html, ISSN 1079-5952

John Kotter and Holger Rathgeber, *Our Iceberg Is Melting: Changing and Succeeding Under Any Conditions*, St. Martin's Press, 2005, ISBN 978-0-312361-98-3

Otto Kroeger, with Janet M. Thuesen, *Type Talk at Work: How the 16 Personality Types Determine Your Success on the Job*, Dell Publishing, 2002, ISBN 978-0-440509-28-8

Elisabeth Kübler-Ross, *On Death and Dying: What the Dying Have to Teach Doctors, Nursers, Clergy and Their Own Families*, Routledge, 2008, ISBN 978-0-415463-99-7

Michael D. Maginn, *Managing in Times of Change: 24 Tools for Managers, Individuals, and Teams*, McGraw-Hill, 2005, ISBN 978-0-071449-11-3

William D. G. Murray, *Give Yourself the Unfair Advantage! A Serious, Practice Guide to Understanding Human Personality That Will Have You Rolling in the Aisles*, Type & Temperament, Inc., 1995, ISBN 978-1-878287-02-1

Isabel Briggs Myers, with Peter B. Myers, *Gifts Differing: Understanding Personality Type*, CPP Books, 1980, ISBN 978-0-891060-74-1

Nick Paumgarten, 'Up and Then Down,' *New Yorker*, 21 April 2008

Jeanne Ray, *Eat Cake*, Shaye Areheart Books, 2003, ISBN 978-0-451211-97-2

Lou Russell and Jeff Feldman, *IT Leadership Alchemy*, Prentice Hall PTR, 2003, ISBN 978-0-130094-03-2

Virginia Satir, John Banmen, Jane Gerber, and Maria Gomori, *The Satir Model: Family Therapy and Beyond*, Science and Behavior Books, Inc., 1991, ISBN 978-0-831400-78-1

Lynne Sharon Schwartz, *The Writing on the Wall*, Counterpoint, 2005, ISBN 978-1-582432-99-1

Rolf Smith, *The 7 Levels of Change: The Guide to Innovation in the World's Largest Corporations*, The Summit Publishing Group, 1997, ISBN 978-1-565302-07-5

Wayne Strider, *Powerful Project Leadership*, Management Concepts, 2002, ISBN 978-1-567261-47-9

Gerald M. Weinberg, *Becoming a Technical Leader: An Organic Problem-Solving Approach*, Dorset House Publishing, 1986, ISBN 978-0-932633-02-6

Gerald M. Weinberg, *Quality Software Management, Vol. 4: Anticipating Change*, Dorset House Publishing, 1997, ISBN 978-0-932633-32-3

Gerald M. Weinberg, *The Secrets of Consulting: A Guide to Giving and Getting Advice Successfully*, Dorset House Publishing, 1985, ISBN 978-0-932633-01-9

Margaret J. Wheatley, *Leadership and the New Science: Discovering Order in a Chaotic World*, Berrett-Koehler Publishers, 1999, ISBN 978-1-574533-40-8

ITG RESOURCES

IT Governance Ltd sources, creates and delivers products and services to meet the real-world, evolving IT governance needs of today's organisations, directors, managers and practitioners. The ITG website (*www.itgovernance.co.uk*) is the international one-stop-shop for corporate and IT governance information, advice, guidance, books, tools, training and consultancy.

IT Governance products are also available, in local currencies, through

www.itgovernanceusa.com, and

www.itgovernanceasia.com.

Pocket Guides

For full details of the entire range of pocket guides, simply follow the links at *www.itgovernance.co.uk/publishing.aspx*.

Toolkits

ITG's unique range of toolkits includes the IT Governance Framework Toolkit, which contains all the tools and guidance that you will need in order to develop and implement an appropriate IT governance framework for your organisation. Full details are at *www.itgovernance.co.uk/ products/519*.

For a free paper on how to use the proprietary CALDER-MOIR IT Governance Framework, and for a free trial version of the toolkit, see *www.itgovernance.co.uk/calder_moir.aspx*.

Best Practice Reports

ITG's new range of Best Practice Reports is now at: *www.itgovernance.co.uk/best-practice-reports.aspx*. These offer you essential, pertinent, expertly researched information on an increasing number of key issues.

Training and Consultancy

IT Governance also offers training and consultancy services across the entire spectrum of disciplines in the information governance arena. Details of training courses can be accessed at *www.itgovernance.co.uk/training.aspx* and descriptions of our consultancy services can be found at *http://www.itgovernance.co.uk/consulting.aspx*.

Why not contact us to see how we could help you and your organisation?

Newsletter

IT governance is one of the hottest topics in business today, not least because it is also the fastest-moving, so what better way to keep up than by subscribing to ITG's free monthly newsletter *Sentinel*? It provides monthly updates and resources across the whole spectrum of IT governance subject matter, including risk management, information security, ITIL and IT service management, project governance, compliance and so much more. Subscribe for your free copy at: *www.itgovernance.co.uk/newsletter.aspx*.

CPSIA information can be obtained at www.ICGtesting.com
225885LV00002B/8/P

9 781905 356942